LifeBoats

LifeBoats

FRIENDS *WITH* PURPOSE

by Jim Ailor

LifeBoats: Friends with Purpose

Copyright © 2013 by Jim Ailor

ISBN: 978-1492900566

Edited by Dara Powers Parker

This work is available for purchase at Amazon.com.

Author's note: Much of what I've learned about LifeBoats (other than what I've experienced first-hand) comes from an audio sermon series by Bill Hybels of Willow Creek Community Church, titled *Enlisting Little Platoons.* Hybel's teachings and terminology have so invaded my own, that I must credit "Platoons" as the main source of the information in this book.

Contents

Man the Boats

I call it a LifeBoat.

Most organizations call it a "small group," or some other such colorless label. This kind of tag really undervalues the essence of the thing. I prefer to title something vividly — give it a name that describes what you're in for. And, man, are you in for a phenomenal journey!

And so I call it a LifeBoat, because it *will* save your life.

If you don't have a LifeBoat, you probably don't know what you're missing. Or maybe I should put it this way: Just you wait until you experience the adventure and camaraderie that is coming your way!

Although I don't like to call it by its literal definition, a LifeBoat is in fact a small group of friends, meeting together with the purpose of spurring one another to grow in Christ.

Now, I know I just described a small group to you; however, you must never call your small groups at church *small groups*. It compels absolutely no one to join. When you paint a verbal

picture of how life-changing a LifeBoat can be — how supportive and loving, how challenging and thriving — you don't want to ruin it with the mental image of people sitting around a table having tea and cookies. Who's got time for that?

So where did I come up with the label LifeBoat? Well, it was in an actual boat that my first significant group — after meeting for months — finally came together, crossed the threshold, and became a real functioning crew. (I'll tell you that story later).

If you're like me (and I hope you're not), you typically read the introduction and/or the first chapter of a book, hoping you'll get the gist and not be required to

read further. So before I lose you, let me give you the bottom line.

First, building a LifeBoat fleet (a small-group ministry) is not so hard. I've watched too many churches make it a lot more complex than it needs to be. In fact, you stifle group growth by complicating it.

It's not hard to accomplish because the concept of LifeBoating is built into our DNA. Evolutionary scientists call humans "social animals," because for the most part we need interaction. It's one of our most basic necessities. Add to that the Christian factor, with which God's love infuses us, and you end up with this deep longing to relate to God's people. Christians want to get close to other believers to see the image of God in them.

Therefore, let me encourage you to keep it simple. Keep the rules minimal. And more than anything, give people permission to do what comes pretty naturally to most.

Christian growth is a team sport. Just like sailing a ship, it's not something we can do very well on our own. God built within us this desire to connect with others. We seek companionship. It's simple, because it's the most natural thing in the world. It's what people want: lifelong, reliable, meaningful relationships. Friendships that will make them better people, and friends who will walk through life with us.

LifeBoating is really about friendship. It's friends with a purpose, and friends are essential to our well-being. Dr. Oz calls them Vitamin F ("F" for *friends*). He points out how research shows that people in secure social circles have less risk of depression and terminal strokes. "If you enjoy Vitamin F constantly, you can be up to thirty years younger than your real age."

It's the warmth of friendship that reduces stress and adds so much to life. Researchers keep finding more and more benefits to a life full of friends.

Now, the difference with these LifeBoat friendships is that they intentionally spur one another in their Christian walk. "To spur" means to urge forward, to encourage, to promote. It is motivation, stimulation, inspiration, and drive.

Yeah, but what about those introverts? Well, some people feel better in very small groups ... like two or three. Others feel more comfortable in a larger group, where they can hide a bit. Again, the rule is to not make rules ... or at least as few as possible. Make sure your folks know it's okay to have a group of two ("me and thee"). Even Jesus gave permission for this when He said, "For where two or three are gathered in My name, there I am with them."

Here are the two main things (and keep the main thing the main thing).

1. The key to effective LifeBoats is purpose, and the right purpose of a LifeBoat is "to spur one another" to grow in Christ. Say it any way you want, but your LifeBoat needs to be about pushing each other to move forward in your relationships with Christ. If LifeBoats know that is their purpose, they will figure out how to do that with very little help. So the church's main job is to keep reminding

DOING LIFE TOGETHER

"Those who accepted his message were baptized, and about three thousand were added to their number that day.

"They devoted themselves to the apostles' teaching and to the fellowship, to the breaking of bread and to prayer. Everyone was filled with awe, and many wonders and miraculous signs were done by the apostles. All the believers were together and had everything in common. Selling their possessions and goods, they gave to anyone as he had need. Every day they continued to meet together in the temple courts. They broke bread in their homes and ate together with glad and sincere hearts, praising God and enjoying the favor of all the people. And the Lord added to their number daily those who were being saved."

—Acts 2:41-47

LifeBoats what their purpose is. Don't let them forget that.

2. The other main responsibility of the church is to keep casting the vision of what a LifeBoat can be. Keep painting that picture of what an ideal LifeBoat looks like. Throughout this book we'll throw you ideas about how to cast that vision.

The LifeBoat Survival Stories throughout are mostly anecdotes from the Life-Boats I've participated in. These will remind you of similar stories from your own experiences. Tell some of my stories in your church, but tell lots of your stories. And ask folks in your church to tell their stories, as well. Not just stories from the LifeBoats in your church, but examples from your groups of friends in years past. This was a LifeBoat too, you just didn't

know what to call it then.

I'll tell you now, the hardest type to "sell" the concept of LifeBoats to are adult males. The "group" idea — i.e., sitting and sharing — is really hard for men to get past. That's one reason I warn against calling your ministry Life Groups, Home Groups, Cell Groups, or anything including the word *group*.

Leonard Sweet, the author and theologian, calls his men's group "Grid Iron," and it meets around Monday-night football games. You might want to call your men's group a *tribe* or a *pack*. One group I know is called "The Cave." Anything with that "Band-of-Brothers," "Fellowship-of-the-Ring" feel to it. Another men's group I know meets at the shooting range. They shoot, talk, and then shoot some more. Meet at the docks, on the golf course, the weight room, after a run, or before a hike or a bike. Just please don't call it a "group."

So what is the biggest challenge for LifeBoats? As I talk to churches with successful small-group ministry, the recurring problem they cite is child care. Surprised? I was. But the logistics of figuring out what to do for LifeBoat families with young children seems to be the major challenge. See pages 57-58 for ideas about how to address the child-care issue.

The second problem is the fear of a LifeBoat turning dysfunctional. Many of the pastors I talk to who don't do small groups in their church say, "Small groups can be toxic. They give people a chance to discredit the church and its leadership, and that can lead to trouble." Their churches miss the wonders and discipleship of Life-Boats because of fear. (For more on this, see "Members with Their Own Agenda" in the Troubleshooting chapter on pages 98-99.)

Other churches respond to this fearful prospect by over-organizing their small groups so there isn't time to gripe and complain; they do this by setting up rigid accountability systems to counteract potential poison. This strategy goes against the keep-it-simple rule and stifles spiritual growth.

There must be a better way to deal with this fear. After all, people talk. The very thought that you can keep people from talking by discouraging small groups is laughable. In reality, it's almost comical watching some church leaders making their moves to keep people from talking. By not establishing LifeBoats in your church, you are not going to stop people from talking. Excessive control will not stop it either; in fact, it may stimulate more negative talk.

I have always found it better to trust God with this fear. Pray it through. Education helps too. Teach people about this

---

LIFEBOAT SURVIVAL STORY
"Never Too Old"

I recently stayed overnight at my mom's house. At the time I write this book, my mother is ninety-three years old but still very involved in relationships; she has more friends than we could ever count, and she is known in her church and community for being well connected.

At dawn the next morning, I caught Mom on the telephone. To be truthful, she is on the phone frequently throughout the day, but who was she calling so early? It was her good friend Maggie, who lives a couple blocks away. I knew it was Maggie, because this is their habit. They talk on the phone several times a week, and get together in person several times, as well.

While I was considering this, it occurred to me that Mom and Maggie have been in a two-person LifeBoat for decades.

This relationship is so important to my mom, because Maggie is Mom's compass. Even though my mother is in her nineties and Maggie is five years older, these two women keep each other young and pointed in the right direction.

Spiritually and emotionally, they need each other. They talk about their Bible studies, about what God is saying to them. They talk about their other relationships and make sure to connect with those friends, too. They keep each other straight. If one is getting too wild and crazy or acting too old and boring, the other will tell her so. They inspire one another to live a life worth living.

This example has taught me that you're never too old for a LifeBoat. You will never outgrow your need for companionship and purpose. It's one of our lives' greatest essentials. No matter how long we live, we will always need our LifeBoat.

unpleasant possibility and show how it is the opposite of what LifeBoats should be about. This foreknowledge will help Life-Boats monitor themselves and also enable them to discern where a conversation is going while they can still change its direction. People often get sucked into messages before they realize what is happening because they have never been taught otherwise. In fact, a healthy church is one in which the congregation speaks up and says, "Hey, we don't talk like that around here. That is not what our church is about. If we have a problem with something, we go talk it out directly with the leader that can do something about it. We don't assault others with our negative dialogue." Changing the culture of a church into a positive environment is what needs to happen. But that won't come about by using obsessive control checks.

LifeBoats: Church & Lifelong

In this book we will be discussing two kinds of LifeBoats: *Church* LifeBoats and *Lifelong* LifeBoats. Most of the time we will generalize the term *LifeBoat*, but the difference between the two kinds is important to grasp.

Church LifeBoats are the small groups that your church helps form. These are but a sip of what a genuine, full-potential, functioning LifeBoat can be. Hopefully, your church is designing their small-group ministry with the intention of helping you find your Lifelong LifeBoat. What would really be nifty is if your Church LifeBoat

happened to be your Lifelong LifeBoat.

As you have probably inferred, your Lifelong LifeBoat is a set of friends that naturally accompany you in your Christian journey, providing support, encouragement, and motivation. These friendships can last a lifetime.

Don't get me wrong — even Lifelong LifeBoats have a life cycle. Usually with Lifelong LifeBoats there is a natural attrition as people move away, or drift away, or die. And new people will become a part of your Lifelong LifeBoat, which is necessary and good. New blood can energize a group, and God often uses new people to lead your crew into new territory and to new insights.

Your Church LifeBoat will be characterized by "program." The meeting will be much more structured. There will be material, announcements, agendas. But despite all that business, your Church Life-Boat will help you discover who you want to LifeBoat with long term.

About This Book...
This book is designed to help churches under 125 in attendance experience remarkable small groups. Most single-staff churches don't have the ability to read book after book and organize a highly complex program. For that reason, you'll notice this book is short, to the point, and makes implementing small groups in your church as easy as possible. Please — *please!* — don't make it harder than it really is. Watch out for mission creep. Remember it was the Pharisees who were inclined to add to the Law. It was Jesus who simply said, "Love one another."

Also, this book may be different than other books about small-group ministry because it views groups as long-term, maybe even lifelong, organisms. It's really about forming lifelong friendships that encourage each other in their walk with Christ. Really, it's walking together through life with Christ.

There are all sorts of groups: Alpha, Recovery, Grief, Parenting, and so on. But this book will stick with groups — LifeBoats — that inspire its members to collaborate, following Christ and supporting one another.

Minimum Requirements to be an Official Church LifeBoat

1. **Must have both a LifeGuard (leader) and a First Mate (an apprentice or LifeGuard-in-training)**

2. **LifeGuard must have completed the training**

3. **Staff approval**

4. **Meets at least twice a month**

5. **Intends to cover the four main components (Caring, Prayer, Bible Study, and Kingdom Work)**

6. **Intends to grow**

The Purpose of LifeBoats

Isn't it a relief to know that we are all in the same boat? That's what LifeBoating is all about — doing life together.

But there is another fundamental upshot that emerges when Christians do life together. It changes us.

You see, the chief purpose of LifeBoats is to spur one another to grow in Christ. This idea comes from Hebrews 10:24-25, which says, "And let us consider how to spur one another on toward love and good deeds not giving up meeting together, as some are in the habit of doing, but encouraging one another — and all the more as you see the Day approaching."

The Church exists not to collect people, but to transform them. A church's Sunday services may attract people and introduce them to Christ. Transforming people, however, usually comes about in the smaller gatherings, where God uses up-close and personal relationships to achieve His goal of changing lives. This is why LifeBoats are so important in the life of a church.

A LifeBoat provides the prime environment for the transformation Jesus Christ intends for every believer. Jesus expects His followers to become like Him. An organized group that by design does not contribute to this goal of growth in Christ may well be a collection of Christians, but it is not an authentic LifeBoat. It might be comparable to a cruise ship, in which all the passengers are relaxing in the hot tub. Contrary to that tempting image, Scripture tells us to "spur" one another on to be better Christians. We need to row, we need to push, we might even need to bail water out of the boat to make it float.

In your LifeBoat, you'll receive the encouragement you need. When you have to make the tough call or push past your limits of comfort, your shipmates will be the ones cheering you on with a smile and reassuring slap on the back.

As the relationships grow deeper and the trust level increases, you'll start to rely on your LifeBoat to help you conquer temptations. You'll find yourself confessing, "There's this girl at the office, and she's got my attention. I need your help here."

There are other byproducts of Life-Boats — secondary purposes, which make them doubly important. They help us to care for individual needs; newcomers are assimilated and connected to the church through relationship, which is the strongest kind of bond; people are discipled; and lay leadership is developed and empowered for ministry. Our main focus, however, is to help each other become all that God created us to be in Christ Jesus.

People who want to grow will find a way to grow. People who don't want to grow, won't. A LifeBoat offers an advantageous setting for spiritual growth, because it will make people want to grow. And they will! Talking about it increases desire and the desire becomes contagious until the whole crew catches the infection.

If you are serious about growing like Christ, nothing will enable you more than being in a LifeBoat. Here, the emphasis is on life — the abundant life that is found in a close relationship with Jesus.

When you first launch a LifeBoat crew, the meetings will start out with ice breakers. The conversation will be superficial, the Bible study straightforward. But as the relationships develop, the sharing and open connection will go deeper and deeper.

At one meeting you'll mention that you would like to be more consistent in spending time each day in God's Word. At the next meeting, a shipmate will lean forward, look you in the eye, and say, "So, how did it go with your daily devotions this week?" That is called accountability.

When the storms of life leave you battered and shipwrecked, this crew will be the first people at your door. And you will be relieved to see them. You will know that they are praying for you, supporting you, and helping in every way possible. As you support the others in your LifeBoat, you'll know that you are doing the work of God, ministering in His name. The love, support, and caring that endures in Life-Boats cannot be found anywhere else. It is a means to bless others, and to be blessed mutually.

Biblical Community

Dr. Bill Donahue writes about the model of discipleship, as practiced by Jesus in his book, *Leading Life-Changing Small Groups*:

Community is a theme that runs throughout Scripture... God has always been calling out a people for Himself, beginning with Israel and continuing with the church. Even when the Jews were dispersed among enemy nations during times of captivity, they organized themselves into groups and ultimately formed synagogues (Jewish communities of worship and teaching) where they could serve one another and carry out their beliefs. It was natural, therefore, for Jesus to develop a community of followers and for Paul, Peter, and other church planters to start "new communities" wherever they went as they proclaimed the gospel. These new communities began as small groups just as Jesus modeled with the twelve disciples.

Throughout the New Testament we see small clusters of Christians banding together. Jesus chose twelve close friends. Paul had Timothy, Luke, Barnabas, and Silas, and he almost never traveled anywhere by himself. Acts 2 shows the early Church meeting together daily, probably in small groups. The Epistles are loaded with references to house churches. Even under persecution, the Christians in Rome stole into that city's sewer system (the catacombs) so they might meet together.

Among the Twelve, Jesus maintained a tighter LifeBoat of three. It was Peter, James, and John. At every major event in His life, you find these three friends. On the Mount of Transfiguration, only Peter, James, and John witnessed Jesus glorified. In Gethsemane, as Jesus faced the reality of his coming crucifixion, he took these three to be close to Him. "My soul is exceedingly sorrowful ... pray with me."

Christians Unite

Christians have been accused of being cluster maniacs. The world is baffled by our need to get together. It seems to them that Sunday morning should be enough. Why do we have to meet during the week, too? "I mean all you do is sit around and talk!" Someone even predicted that if you put ten Christians in a room with a thousand people, the ten would find each other, gather in a corner, and start talking excitedly — "sharing" their Christian adventures with each other — within an hour.

It's what theologians call *community*. It's the feeling of belonging, of being interwoven. It's got to do with relationships, and it's in relationships where Christianity is proved out. Jesus said it this way: "They will know you are My followers by your love for one another." Relationship is where the rubber meets the road for a believer.

Joyce told her preacher, "I couldn't believe you did a 48-week sermon series on relationships last year. I was really getting bored with the topic and wondering, 'Why in the world?' But I have now begun to understand that *it is all about relationships.*"

Another word theologians use is *fellowship*. It's the greek word *koinia*, a very strong word. Dick Woodward — founder of the Mini Bible College and Williamsburg Community Chapel — defines fellowship as "two fellows in the same ship." Then he continues to explain that fellowship is not merely sitting in the same boat . . . you need to pick up an oar and row! LifeBoats are fellowship — a few fellows in the same ship.

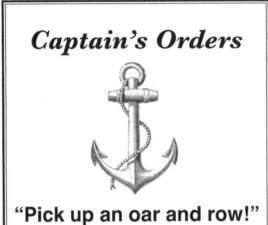

Captain's Orders

"Pick up an oar and row!"

Discipleship

During the past few years, at any gathering of church leaders, you would hear everyone talking about discipleship. It's not a buzz word, but it is the concern of most church leaders these days. Since the emergence of the REVEAL Spiritual Life Survey, more and more research suggests that

what we are doing in churches is not creating disciples. Active churchgoers are not growing in the Lord, even though they are faithful in church attendance, Bible studies, and prayer meetings. We're doing an excellent job of imparting knowledge and getting people involved in church work, but personal, spiritual growth is unfortunately not the byproduct.

And yet the disciplines that produce growth have not changed. If you want to grow spiritually, you must adopt five habits.

A Consistent Quiet Time. This is when you spend one-on-one time with the Lord, with minimum distractions, so your relationship with God can develop. This would include Bible study and prayer.

Corporate Worship. This is when you join with others and pour your heart out to God in worship and adoration. As we express our love for God and proclaim His praises, God "inhabits" our worship, and our relationship with Him deepens. We also absorb strength from the other believers with whom we are worshiping.

Sharing Your Faith. Besides benefiting the one you are sharing with, your faith is strengthened as you verbalize what you believe to someone who doesn't believe like you do. Also, as the Holy Spirit works through you, your relationship with God

matures and your faith increases.

Kingdom Service. As you go about doing God's work (ministering to the hurting or advancing His redemptive plan), God comes to work alongside you. Don't think of Kingdom service as doing something for God, but rather working *with* God (actually, He does the hard part). Just as you build relationships with the people you work with, so your relationship with God gets better as you work with Him.

A LifeBoat. Of these five elements, this is the most important, because your LifeBoat will push you to pursue the other four.

Bill Hybels, the pastor of Willow Creek Community Church, said, "Sooner or later, every serious Christian wakens to the fact that they cannot reach their full spiritual potential without the involvement of other people."

For a while, we think that if we can just muster the will power to wake up early each morning to spend time with God — if we can make ourselves attend church every Sunday — then we will eventually grow to be spiritual giants. But it's only a matter of time before we start putting on spiritual airs and end up talking like we're further along than we really are. We start taking shortcuts and soon we're slipping into sin. We lose our fire. We get distracted. We shun the spiritual challenges we ought to be jumping at. We settle for nominal Christianity, or worse.

Doing this on your own is not the way it's supposed to be. Sure Paul, even Jesus had their moments when they came up against life's hardships alone. But for the most part, they surrounded themselves with other believers. In 2 Timothy 4, we hear Paul longing to have his friends with him; he doesn't want to face his trial alone.

Solo Christians feel isolated, estranged. Without the accountability, the counsel, and the motivation of a LifeBoat, living out the Christian experience is exhausting.

You were not meant to do life by yourself. God said of Adam, "It is not good for the man to be alone."

When I was a pastor, I always enjoyed getting together with a group of other pastors. I'd frequently catch the zeal of an excited pastor, or one would say something deep that I could chew on for days. Furthermore, we as a group were able to multiply our reading and our study, because we shared what we saw with each other. My LifeBoat is the very same; I catch someone's enthusiasm, someone's insight, someone's example.

Christianity is a co-op. What makes us think we can reach exotic spiritual destinations by ourselves? A LifeBoat can take you past the boundaries that limit you.

Relationships

I tend to think of most church fellowship activities as a chance to meet potential LifeBoat crews and sift through the prospects to discover who I'll be LifeBoating with. The church dinners, baseball teams, and class outings rarely get past surface relationships. But these pursuits do give you the opportunity to meet fellow believers with whom you might want to go deeper.

All LifeBoats embark by skimming the surface. But in our busy world, people have less and less time or patience for surface relationships. Social networking is all about shallow associations. People can handle

that sort of relationship while on the run. But Facebook, Twitter, and LinkedIn seem to produce a hankering for something more — for real relationships rather than pseudo-connection. We're all looking for lifelong friendships and people we can count on.

A LifeBoat's Life Cycle

How long will it take for a LifeBoat to cross the threshold past surface encounters? That usually depends on how often it meets. A LifeBoat that gathers once a month will take six times as long to gel as the one that meets weekly. Now, if you're doing the math, you'd guess it would take *four* times as long. But the ground lost between meetings contributes to the time frame, stretching the process of development. If you want to jumpstart your relationships, a good idea is to arrange a long weekend together at a retreat center, a campground, or a resort.

How long is a LifeBoat supposed to last? Hopefully a long time. I would strive for lifelong friendships. A thriving Life-Boat might meet weekly for a couple of years. Then after the relationship is fully established, it might reduce to monthly, then quarterly gatherings. But those widespread meetings are extended. The crew mates will spend the better part of a day together. Once the relationships are solid, a weekend every few months will do. Of course, when a crisis arrises, a get-together will form quickly and spontaneously.

You probably have a friend who when you see them — even after an absence of several years — it's like you were never apart. Things sort of pick up where you

left off. Well, that is the nature of an established relationship. When you get there, you can go to quarterly gatherings, or even biannually. That's appropriate for LifeBoats in which some of the members have moved out of state.

God Uses Relationships

Part of my job currently is putting pastors together. It's astounding to watch once a friendship is formed and trust established what God can do with that. Ministry is born of such bonds. I'd say the most significant ministries in history started with a friendship and a discovery of a common passion, a common conviction, a heart for a common need, and/or a common vision.

JESUS' LIFEBOAT

"Then Jesus went with his disciples to a place called Gethsemane, and he said to them, 'Sit here while I go over there and pray.' He took Peter and the two sons of Zebedee along with him, and he began to be sorrowful and troubled. Then he said to them, 'My soul is overwhelmed with sorrow to the point of death. Stay here and keep watch with me.' Going a little farther, he fell with his face to the ground and prayed, 'My Father, if it is possible, may this cup be taken from me. Yet not as I will, but as you will.' "

—Matthew 26:36-39

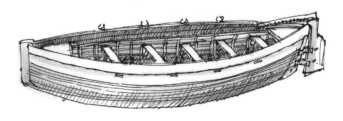

CASTING THE VISION
"Obeying One-Another Commands"

The New Testament is full of "one-another" passages that include directions for living with others. It would be impossible to obey these commands within a large crowd, but it is quite doable with a small group. Here is just a sampling of some one-another commandments:

"Love one another..."

"Be devoted to one another..."

"Live in harmony with one another..."

"Accept one another..."

"Instruct one another..."

"Serve one another..."

"Carry one another's burdens..."

"Be patient, bearing one another in love..."

"Be kind and compassionate to one another..."

"Forgiving one another..."

"Submit to one another out of reverence for Christ..."

"Teach one another..."

"Admonish one another..."

"Encourage one another..."

"Spur one another on toward love and good deeds..."

"Confess your sins to one another..."

"Pray for one another..."

Life in a LifeBoat

It is recommended that LifeBoats meet at least twice a month. Weekly is preferable. The idea is to reach that pivotal threshold, that juncture at which the group gels. This is where the relationships go beyond the surface and when the trust levels are secure. This is when the power of the relationships will propel the passion that makes LifeBoats effective.

The LifeBoats that meet every other week take twice as long to develop and twice as long to build lasting relationships. So you can image how long it would take a monthly LifeBoat to reach that juncture. The time frame is expanded further when every time you meet you must review what was covered in the last meeting because memories have begun to blur. One way to speed up the development process is to schedule a multi-day retreat. Youth workers will tell you that you can accomplish more to build the intensity of your student ministry in one three-day retreat than you can all year with one hour on Sunday morning.

> *"A lot of people ask me, if I were shipwrecked, and could have only one book, what would it be? I always answer,* How to Build a Boat.*"*
>
> —*Stephen Wright*

Times of Ecstasy

Some people imagine small-group meetings to be serious occasions. But there have been times in my LifeBoat when I laughed so hard, I almost fell overboard! Once Tom staggered from the room doubled over, his sides aching so from laughing, he felt he had to get out of the room and away from the source before he split open.

We've grown so comfortable with each other, so confident that we have the unconditional love and respect of all in the room, that we can joke, tease, and poke fun at one another and all it produces is riotous laughter. We've gotten past the point where we worry about impressing each other. We can let our hair down. We've lost most of our inhibitions, and we feel so free in each other's company that we very well might laugh until we cry.

And LifeBoating isn't just sitting around and talking. It's adventure — doing life together. It's working together, spurring each other on toward love and good deeds, as the writer of Hebrews says it.

Churchy folks might use words like *missions* or *ministry*. Yes, we're serving somebody or helping each other out with a project. But for us, it's just another adventure — time to do something together and enjoy being with one another.

Okay, I'll admit that lots of times we just find something fun to do. No mission or ministry included. Maybe it's a hike, a picnic, or a pool party.

The reminiscing sessions are the best. "You remember that time when..." the conversation will start. Then another memory will piggyback on that one, then another. It really gets good when a new guy is around, and we have to catch him up to speed on what a grand LifeBoat he's stumbled into.

Nothing helps define a LifeBoat like its stories.

When it comes to LifeBoating, never neglect the fun factor. And tell your stories until you get really good at it.

Times of Pain

The opposite of "Times of Ecstasy" is the "Times of Pain." I can guarantee that there will be misunderstandings, harsh words, and relational mistakes. The pattern seems to go like this: When a LifeBoat first forms, conversations stay superficial and trust levels start low. This beginning is followed by a period when conversations go beyond the surface, and appreciation for the other crew mates develops; but the relationships haven't been tested, and so there is still a level of insecurity. The result is bruised egos. Pointed words, even off-handed remarks, are not perceived as coming out of genuine love and concern. The tone of voice may sound supportive, but that love has not been proved. The consequence is hurt feelings.

As the trust levels rise, as we become more aware that we are loved and our well-being is the LifeBoats's objective, the insecurity begins to wane. It's at this stage that jabs are taken more as signs of affection rather than attacks.

Learning conflict resolution is a key

skill of a disciple of Christ. And so in our LifeBoats, learning to work through those hurtful moments is important to our spiritual growth.

Another source of pain in a LifeBoat comes when a shipmate is hurting. You have come to truly care about this individual and your lives have become entwined. Pacing in the waiting room, shuffling through the doors of the funeral home, and sitting on the edge of the hospital bed can wrench our hearts with pain as we experience what our friend is going through.

As you learn to "love one another," the "other's" pain becomes your pain.

I'll never forget the pain I felt the night that Timothy called four of us to his apartment to tell us he was bailing. He was throwing in the towel — not only on the seminary we were all enrolled in, but on Christianity altogether. He'd gathered us together to tell us not to follow him or try to contact him. He had realized that he wouldn't be able to give up on Christianity and live his life the way he wanted to if his LifeBoat were tagging along. It was goodbye. And it was final. To this day, the four of us have no idea where he is or what happened to him.

There I was, a seasoned seminary student, and I didn't know what to say to convince Tim not to bail. Theology and apologetics failed me in that moment. All I remember thinking as we walked away was, *Once we were five, and now we are four.* It was a heavy, traumatic emotion.

Losing a member of your crew — however it might happen — is agonizing. Be prepared for heartbreak.

LIFEBOAT SURVIVAL STORY
"Blind Spot"

I guess people had tried to tell me before. But my defensive mechanisms were well developed, fine tuned, and very effective. I had found ways to mentally block out any reference to this thing inside me that I didn't want to see. That's why they call it a blind spot. I couldn't see it ... but everyone else around me could.

I was a youth director at the time, and my LifeBoat was helping to chaperone a church youth outing to the beach. I was calling the shots because, after all, I was the leader. We had surrounded my little red Volkswagen Beetle and were trying to decide what to do next. As the leader, I had to put my foot down. Everyone wanted to head south to the amusement park, but I thought we should head down the beach the other way. The tension mounted, and I finally had to cut the discussion short and order everyone north. After I turned to leave, one of my LifeBoat buddies wrote in large letters, "EGO FREAK," across the top of my car in the dust.

When we returned hours later and I saw the proclamation, my first thought wasn't, "Man, I need to wash my car." Instead, I exploded. I wheeled around and saw Terry staring at me with a sly smile on his face. I immediately knew he was the culprit.

The youth group kids were climbing into the vans, but my LifeBoat crew was moving toward me. At first I mistook it as an attack. But in the back of my mind, I knew without a question that these guys cared for me. They'd even said they'd take a bullet for me (though I doubted they'd take a head or chest shot ... a superficial shoulder hit for sure, though). I was mad as a hornet, but there they stood to confront me. They weren't going anywhere. I could yell, call them names, throw out insults, but they were going to remain by my side. If I ran, they'd come after me, and I somehow sensed that.

Eventually I cooled off enough to see straight. It was a good thing, because my shipmates knew I needed to see this ugly streak in myself. If I was ever going to be an effective leader that people followed willingly, I was going to have to confront this demon.

Over the next few months, they hung in there. To me it felt like they were pinning me against the ground, forcing me look at this monstrosity about myself. All the while, I knew they were going to be my friends whether I changed or not. They loved me just the way I was, and they were going to love me through even this.

Don't get me wrong — I'm still an ego freak. I've since learned to cope with it better, thank heaven, and even manage it to some degree. I'm perhaps more polite about it, more socially correct. I can back away from it at times, and force my way through it at others. I try not to act on it, if I can help it. I prayed *through* it really — prayed it through to the other side with my mates.

If they hadn't made me stare it down, it probably would have grown. It may have ruined me in the long run. Just knowing it's there inside of me helps me move past it.

That kind of brutal intervention settles gentler when it's from people who love you.

Times of Confrontation

A pastor friend once warned me, "When a congregant opens the conversation with, 'Pastor, you know I love you, but...' dive for cover." He then yelled in a military officer's pitch, "In coming!" followed by, "BOOM, BOOM, BOOM!"

For most of us, receiving criticism is distressing. There are some people who are very secure in who they are and can evaluate criticism unemotionally, with matter-of-fact impassivity. There are others who just don't care what other people think, so criticism bounces right off. But for most of us, hearing criticism is hurtful and upsetting. At times it can cut right to the bone.

There are reasons we have blind spots in our self-perceptions. There are things that we are not ready to deal with and our psyches protect us from the reality. We just don't want to see those things about ourselves. Sometimes no matter who is confronting us, we can get pretty touchy about those delicate areas.

It is easier to take, however, from people who love us. And the truth is we need to process how others perceive us.

When Paul told us to correct one another in love, he didn't mean to begin every criticism with "I love you." He meant that you are not allowed to give constructive criticism until you have proved your love — until the person you want to correct is convinced that you love them and will continue to love them whether they change or not.

In my LifeBoat, we've worked on our language, our finances, and our time management. We've been boating together for a long time, so the list of things we've worked on is long, as we tweak each other here and there.

Not very often — seldom in fact — comes the all-out confrontation. This happens when the LifeBoat finally confronts the thing about you that you can't see but is driving everyone around you crazy. It can rock your world.

(See the section on "Accountability," pages 51-52.)

Times of Support

Who do you call when a problem lands at your doorstep at two o'clock in the morning? Okay ... who do you call *after* you call 911? Many people I ask that question to stare at me for a long while, then admit, "I don't know who I'd call. Maybe my pastor."

Last week I talked to a man who had been away on a men's retreat; it had affected him deeply. He told me how one speaker after another stood and recounted the trouble they'd had, some of their own making. The one theme, obviously unplanned, that he heard repeat itself went like this: "I didn't know who to turn to. I didn't know who to call for help. I didn't know anyone I could talk this thing out with. I was alone. I only had God. I had to depend on Him, I had no other choice."

This is what God was trying to save us from when He created LifeBoats. We are not meant to go through life alone. Too many of us, for whatever reason, skip building those honest, open, love-saturated relationships. And when our world collapses, we find ourselves alone at sea with no LifeBoat in sight.

One category of Christians I'm especially concerned about are pastors. I know so many pastors who have spent all their time sustaining others, and yet their only support system is their spouse. Their only LifeBoat is their family. Too often I've watched them slip and ruin their marriage in a single day, or seen their kids go off the rails, or heard that their spouse is tired of it all. To whom do they turn?

So who do you call when you get the phone call that changes your life? When the police officer shows up at your door with the chaplain? After hearing the diagnosis from your doctor?

Once your LifeBoat is established — when you start seeing your crew more as friends than members of a group you attend — they will be who you call. When you get that bad news, they will be the first at your door. And believe me, you'll be glad to see them.

Some of your crew mates, the ones you're closest to, will sit with you. You won't feel the need to entertain them or even talk to them if you don't feel like it. They'll just be with you, letting you know you're loved. Others in the LifeBoat will take care of things. I've seen LifeBoats make arrangements for the hospital bed to be delivered and then rearrange the room and get it set up. I've seen LifeBoats cut the grass, vacuum the house, and clean the bathrooms, because they know people will be coming by. I've seen them stand at the door and let friends in and keep the reporters out.

LifeBoats figure out all the ways to keep you afloat. They'll do whatever it takes to take the sting out of the situation.

I've gotten that phone call. I've had my legs cut out from under me. And, oh, how I appreciated my LifeBoat — how I needed them. My mates have always come through for me.

LIFEBOAT SURVIVAL STORY
"Neighborhood Crisis"

We lived in one of those neighborhoods comprised of hundreds of houses stacked close together. The main road through the 'hood was a three-mile loop. Although it looked like a peaceful side street, it was dangerous because cars took it too fast and the kids weren't scared of it. One terrible afternoon, a nine-year-old girl rode her bike out of her driveway and into the street. She was killed instantly.

They lived several blocks from us, but the neighbors kept pushing me to do some-

LIFEBOAT SURVIVAL STORY *continued*

thing, since I was the teaching pastor at a local church. "You're a minister. You need to go visit them." I didn't want to go. Who would? I resisted for a couple of hours, but then I got the word that the family were members of our church. The church was large, I was new, and I didn't think I had met them.

I remember walking up the sidewalk thinking that I had nothing to offer these poor people. If only I had a magic wand to wave or a pill to swallow or a time-rewind button.

When I neared the property, my perspective aligned. I recognized right away that this couple had a LifeBoat. One of the crew was cutting the grass and cleaning up the yard. Another man stood at the door greeting folks. Two women worked in the kitchen, taking the food people brought and organizing it. They'd brought drinks, paper plates and cups, and were making coffee. (Later I found out that they'd even brought toilet paper just in case the family's supply was low.)

The mother was being comforted by two LifeBoat friends in the living room. The father sat in the lounge chair in the den talking nonstop to two men from his LifeBoat; he obviously had a good relationship with these fellows and felt comfortable spilling his guts. The most touching scene was in the dining room, where a woman was helping the six-year-old brother write a note to his sister. I heard that later they tied the note to a bundle of helium balloons and let them float up to heaven.

As I walked home that day, I thanked God that this family had taken the time to involve themselves with a LifeBoat. Through those relationships, God was going to meet their emotional and spiritual needs, much more than I could. All I had was some book learning and some theology and a title that said I was meant to minister to people.

Friendships are better than positions and degrees. Much, much better.

Times of Affirmation

He leaned forward and we locked eyes. "It wasn't easy and it hurt. But *you* did the right thing, man. You stood firm when others would have shrunk back. I'm proud to call you friend."

My spirit soared within me. I had Life-Boated long enough with this guy to know he wouldn't pull my leg. He had called me out when he thought I was heading down the wrong path. He had said, "Think again," when he was questioning my mo-

tives. So now I knew he wasn't blowing smoke. He meant it.

In life, we are always second guessing ourselves ... as we probably should. But the honest appraisal from a shipmate who knows your frailties can push you past the self-doubting to do the right thing.

Being part of a LifeBoat that knows your quirks yet likes you anyway is invaluable to your self-image. Oh sure, they'll work on your weak spots ... but they will also strengthen your strengths.

Times of Guidance

I often use my LifeBoat as a confirmation of God's leading. You see, it's important for me to wrestle with finding God's will. The process of seeking His mind in a matter helps develop the mind of Christ in me. That's something I need to do on my own. But my LifeBoat can confirm a leading.

I'll say something like, "I've been seeking God's direction, and I think He is leading me to do this. Will you take some time and pray this through with me? If you sense the same thing I'm sensing, then that will confirm it for me. If not, then I better head back to the prayer room and listen again."

Or I may say, "Here's what I think I'm supposed to do... Do you detect any red flags in this plan?"

At other times I don't trust my judgment, so I turn to my LifeBoat to help me figure out the options. My LifeBoat can help me pinpoint the warning signs I should be seeing.

The grief counselors will tell a widow or widower after their spouse has died, "Don't make any major decisions for at least a year." But the truth is that they have a lot of decisions they must make right away — major decisions at that. It's times like these when a band of believers who knows you well can help you see clearly. After all, they know your strengths, your talents, your gifts, your passions, your weaknesses. They know the things you hate and the stuff you love. They have watched your face light up when you talk about certain things and they've watched you get bored quickly when the conversation has turned to other things.

"I've been offered this job... Can you see me in that role?" If the mates all respond in unison, "That ain't you, bro!" Don't take the job!

When you're at a major crossroads, the crew can help you sort things out. When you're at a point of grief, when the roof caved in, when life has turned so chaotic that you can't see straight, they'll come alongside you and steer you through the clutter.

There comes a time when we need help just to see our way in the dark. A LifeBoat is a brilliant lighthouse, shining the beam ahead to steer a course through potential peril and shadow.

Times of Mentoring

I was nineteen, in college, and just starting life as an adult. I had crossed the line of faith the year before. As a teen I hadn't paid much attention to how believers lived, dated, or did family life. I had some stereotypes in my mind, but those images didn't seem to fit reality. Now my faith was somewhat zealous and I wanted to please my Lord, but I was unsure how it all worked.

Enter Wayne and Betty. They were twelve years older than me, married, and had two daughters, one eight and one eleven. They said, "Why don't you come live with us for a year. We're believers, so

you can see how we do it. You'll see firsthand how we relate as a married couple and how we raise our kids. You can watch us live it out."

I turned them down ... kinda. I didn't move in, but I was at their house four or five times a week. Especially around dinnertime (single college boy — you know how that works). My friend Gary was usually with me.

They modeled for Gary and me what it was like to live out their Christianity. I saw them argue (I hadn't known Christians did that). Saw them balance work, family, and serving God. I saw them love people I sure didn't want to love. I saw them steal away to pray. Caught them reading the Word. Watched from a polite distance when they corrected their kids.

The four of us were a kind of LifeBoat, but we didn't know what it was back then. We often chatted late into the night about spiritual things and life things. They modeled it well.

Wayne and Betty were showing us the ropes. They were mentoring.

Mentoring is when a more mature believer takes a novice under their wing and shows them the ropes. LifeBoats are a prime setting for mentoring. In a group setting you end up with multiple mentors and multiple cadets. Also, the cadet gets to watch the mentors relate to their LifeBoat, as they spur their crew members to grow in Christ.

In the scriptures we see Moses mentor Joshua and Aaron, Elijah mentor Elisha, Paul mentor Timothy and Titus, Barnabas mentor John Mark, and the list goes on.

This process basically involves letting a young believer into your life. It's allowing the novice to watch you pray; watch you get a hold of God; watch you serve our Lord. It's sitting around the campfire telling your Christian war stories — the hard times, the good times ... the glory of battle.

The process usually begins with the mentor being more mature in the things of the Lord. But as time goes on, the cadet grows and becomes your equal, your peer. One day, you'll find yourself asking the one you've mentored for advice, and you'll know that your relationship has changed.

Mentoring Tip No. 1: When looking for a mentor, find somebody who isn't too far ahead of you. Look for a believer with more zeal (more energy) for the Lord than you have. Look for a mentor who is positive, not the individual who is prone to tell you all the bad stuff of life. Look for a mentor who loves life and tries to live it to the fullest.

Mentoring Tip No. 2: Seldom will a younger believer ask for a mentor. So it's important that you initiate the process. Simply invite a younger believer to do something with you. Let the relationship develop naturally. This is also easier with others in a LifeBoat.

Mentoring Tip No. 3: Look for the "Aristotle Stamp" in an individual. That is who you want to mentor. (See the LifeBoat Survival Story: "Aristotle Stamp" on pages 65-66.)

Mentoring Tip No. 4: Encouragement and approval is key. As a mentor, it's important that you convey to the cadet that they have what it takes.

Times of Coaching

Coaching is a popular concept these days with executive coaches for the CEOs of big companies, and life coaches for us more regular folk, who just want to make sure we're taking full advantage of life. But the coaching that happens in a LifeBoat

An executive coach asks the CEO lots of questions and listens for key points in the answers. So in your LifeBoat, a lot of the questions and comments will be about spiritual growth:

❖ What's the one thing that would most help you be closer to God? A more consistent prayer life? A better Bible understanding? A more receptive attitude in corporate worship? A better approach to sharing your faith?

❖ How is a theology class going to help? That will just confuse the issues. Plus, it's not about information, it's about relationship. So convince me.

❖ How can we as a crew help you with that? How can we support you as you take that on?

❖ Is there anything we can do as a group that would push us all forward?

❖ Let's nail down a plan. A step-by-step process.

❖ Okay, I usually don't get up that early, but if that is best for you, then I'll get up early every day this week. I'll call you at 6:30 a.m. on the dot, and we'll pray together about this one thing.

is a mite different. For one, it's a group thing. Two, the coaches all know you fairly well. They already have a sense of who you are, what makes you *you*, and what you're about. Three, you're coaching each other, so they are taking your advice and you are taking theirs (that just seems more fair). And four, this coaching is about how to grow in your walk with Christ, so it's a discipling thing.

At times you'll think you're meeting with a boardroom full of spiritual coaches. It will be like a team of doctors performing a case study on a patient to determine the best course of action. Thus your team of spiritual coaches will help you figure out your next moves.

The difference is that these coaches pray you through every step of the way.

A life coach helps you pinpoint what you want to accomplish and then helps you form a plan (with benchmarks) to get there. In the same way, your LifeBoat helps you figure out what the next level in your spiritual growth will look like and helps you plan steps to get there.

Seekers Welcome

So what if you're a seeker? Would you be welcome in a LifeBoat? Is a LifeBoat an option for somebody who is just checking out this Christianity stuff? Would there be any benefit for a seeker who hasn't crossed the line of faith yet but is interested?

There is no better way to see Christianity up close than within a LifeBoat. Sure, you can read and study Christianity in books or listen to preachers in front of a large sanctuary or on TV. But the big questions for most seekers are, *Does it work? Is it real? And what's involved?*

The answer to those questions are best answered by watching people live it out — watching people struggle to incorporate it into their lives. In a LifeBoat, you will get to see Christians pray. You'll hear in their voices if they are really talking to the unseen God or just being religious. And you'll know if their prayers get answered.

It's hard to judge a person's motives from a distance. But as you get to know your LifeBoat crew, you'll see the good and the bad. You'll get to see just how forgiven your shipmates are and why they need a Savior. And from time to time, you'll also get to glimpse the image of God in them.

Besides all that, it will be good for the LifeBoat to hear from someone who doesn't see the world through the same filter.

Most people know that spirituality is an important aspect of life that needs developing. In a LifeBoat, you can get serious about spirituality. You'll hear common-sense principles that will work no matter what your faith is. Most will want to participate in the service projects that help people. You will enjoy caring for the hurting in the group, and you will love being cared for. You will be delighted at the friendships that will develop.

Tip: If you're the seeker, be honest and up front about that. Agree where you can and disagree where you need to. If you're a believer in a group with a seeker, don't be judgmental and don't put on a show. Most people can spot a fake instantly, so be honest and check the airs at the door.

PRAYER FOR LIFEBOATS

O Maker of the Mighty Deep
Whereon our vessels fare,
Above our life's adventure keep
Thy faithful watch and care.
In Thee we trust, whate'er befall;
Thy sea is great, our boats are small.

We know not where the secret tides
Will help us or delay;
Nor where the lurking tempest hides,
Nor where the fogs are gray:
We trust in Thee, whate'er befall;
Thy sea is great, our boats are small.
— **"Voyagers" by Henry van Dyke**

LifeBoat Officers

A LifeBoat's leadership team is made up of the LifeGuard (the LifeBoat leader), the First Mate (an apprentice, or LifeGuard-in-training), the Steward (host or hostess), and the Bosun (who will oversee several LifeBoats). The LifeGuard, First Mate, and Bosun lead the individual LifeBoat in fulfilling its goals.

The LifeGuard

Each LifeBoat needs a LifeGuard, their fearless leader. They are the spark plug that fires energy to the engine. They make sure it works. At many churches, the LifeGuard is considered the most strategic

> ### PREPARING OTHERS
> "He appointed twelve—designating them apostles—that they might be with him and that he might send them out to preach."
> —Mark 3:14

position in the congregation. That is why churches will do everything possible to train and equip these leaders.

None of us possesses all the qualifications of Christian leadership. But we expect our leaders to be actively pursuing growth toward Christ-likeness. As a Life-Guard, you need to understand the areas in which you need to grow, and you and your Bosun should make a plan to help

you grow in those areas. You'll want to develop both in character and in competence to be a quality leader.

QUALIFICATIONS FOR LIFEGUARDS

A Passion to follow Christ.
Ephesians 4:13

A Heart to shepherd people.
Matthew 9:36-38

An Ability to guide a group.
Matthew 4:19; Acts 6:1-7

A Temperament to lead people.
Acts 6:2

A Commitment to do what it takes.
Romans 12:1-2; 16:3-4

A Capacity to serve and provide care.
1 Timothy 3:4-5,12

LifeGuard Tip No. 1
PRAY FOR YOUR CREW

Pray for your crew regularly. As their leader, your chief duty is to cover the crew with prayer. Lift your shipmates up individually and be specific in your requests.

One LifeGuard told me he has seven crew members, so he prays for one each day of the week. "I pray for Pete every Monday, Julie every Tuesday, Charlie every Wednesday..." and so on.

I like to write out a prayer for each mate in my LifeBoat. Then I pray that prayer regularly for them. Using a word processor makes it easy to change the prayer as their situations change and as I see more clearly what God is doing in their lives. Here is a shortened version of the one I prayed this morning (I've changed the names):

> *Dear Lord,*
> *I want to thank you for John — for the special way You made him and for the great future you have planned for him. I especially love the way I can see the image of You in him. He seems to have a natural ability for leadership. I notice how the others in the LifeBoat seem to perk up*

QUALIFIED LEADERS

"It is a true saying that if a man wants to be a pastor he has a good ambition. For a pastor must be a good man whose life cannot be spoken against. He must have only one wife, and he must be hard working and thoughtful, orderly, and full of good deeds. He must enjoy having guests in his home and must be a good Bible teacher. He must not be a drinker or quarrelsome, but he must be gentle and kind and not be one who loves money. He must have a well-behaved family, with children who obey quickly and quietly. For if a man can't make his own little family behave, how can he help the whole church?

"The pastor must not be a new Christian because he might be proud of being chosen so soon, and pride comes before a fall. (Satan's downfall is an example.) Also, he must be well spoken of by people outside the church—those who aren't Christians—so that Satan can't trap him with many accusations and leave him without freedom to lead his flock."

—1 Timothy 3:1-7

and listen more intently when he talks and how readily they take his suggestions. So I pray that you will keep developing that within him and help me see how I can help in the process.

I do want to pray about the pain I see in his life. He's really been through the wringer — a rough childhood and a boatload of marital problems. God, he seems to be intent on doing it right, but he never saw it modeled to him growing up. We both know his blind spot, that part of him that he can't see yet. I'm trusting you to open his eyes to that when the timing is right and when he is ready.

Bless him Lord with every spiritual blessing.

Amen.

LifeGuard Tip No. 2
NO TALKING HEAD

Television producers say the worst kind of show is the one with the "talking head." That's when all you hear and see for most of the program is one person talking. That's why even news shows have transitioned to multiple anchors with plenty of video clips.

The same rule applies to LifeBoats. A LifeGuard doing all the talking is not a good leader. Ask questions that are open-ended and then wait for an answer. Don't be afraid of silence. Your job is to draw people out, not entertain. The best Life-Guards I've seen know how to get people talking to each other, rather than everyone dialoging with the leader.

Two tricks I use to stifle myself are as follows: (1) Keep asking myself, *Why am I talking?* and (2) I recruit someone in the LifeBoat, usually my First Mate, to ask follow-up questions. I'll open the discussion part of our meeting by posing the discussion question. *Wait for it, wait for it...* Finally somebody will give a quick answer. Then my First Mate will ask, "What did you mean by that?" or "How did that make you feel?" Perhaps, "Can you fill that out for us some?" or "Can anybody else relate to that?"

THE LIFEGUARD'S
JOB DESCRIPTION

1. Confess that Jesus Christ is Lord, regard the Bible as your authoritative guide to your faith and life, and be a participating member of the church.

2. Take the training.

3. Build a leadership team and develop that leadership (you, a First Mate, and a Steward).

4. Conduct the meetings.

5. Shepherd the members of your Life Boat. (Pray, show concern, serve them, create a safe place for them to share.)

6. Attend the quarterly LifeGuard meetings.

7. Be accountable to your Bosun. Let him/her know what stage your LifeBoat is in; which of the four major components you are emphasizing. Get his/her input and permission for material (if any) you want to use.

LifeGuard Tip No. 3
DON'T KNOW THE ANSWERS

The biggest obstacle when a pastor is leading a LifeBoat is that people will naturally suppose he or she has all the answers. After all, they've been to seminary and therefore know all the answers to life... NOT! And yet people tend to defer to the guy with the position or degree. They may answer the question, but then they look to the pastor for approval. "Is that right?"

A LifeGuard needs to sincerely look to the crew for the answers, and not be an answer man.

"Boy, that's a hard one... Anybody got a clue on how to approach that?" "I wrestle with that issue too. How do you guys look at it?"

And don't be afraid to say, "I don't know."

LifeGuard Tip No. 4
EMPOWER, EMPOWER, EMPOWER

At work I recruited an assistant to help me answer my emails, fill out forms and reports, and take care of phone calls. My team was giving me a hard time about this. So I replied with mock-confusion, "So what you're saying is that leadership is doing everything yourself?" They haven't mentioned it since. (I usually don't win arguments that easily. Usually I'm the one going home scratching my head.)

Be aware that leadership is *not* doing everything yourself. In fact, a good leader is one who hates to do the things somebody else can do. I'm not talking about being lazy; I'm talking about empowering people.

LifeGuard Tip No. 5
DON'T ASSUME SALVATION

Here's a sad story. The pastor that followed me at one of my churches asked me for any hints I might give him soon after he took the position. I suggested that he not assume that the church leaders were Christians.

"I strongly suggest," I said, "you take advantage of being new. Ask the salvation questions first. In your initial conversations with your leaders, ask them how they came to know Christ or when they crossed the line of faith. If you do that within the first six months, it won't offend them, because you don't know them yet. You're just checking and not wanting to assume anything. But if you wait six months and then ask, they'll be offended that you might think they don't know Christ."

Eighteen months later, he told me that he wished he had taken my advice. "I doubt if half of them have a relationship with Jesus. They seemed so nice at first, so Christian. How could someone even become a church leader and not have a saving knowledge of Christ? I just assumed they were believers. But as time has gone by, their true colors have come out. I just don't see the love of God in them at all. I doubt if some of them even know Jesus."

As a LifeBoat leader, you need to ask the salvation questions early. Don't assume it. Study the Gospel and the plan of salvation as a group. Have folks tell their faith story. I've come to appreciate this question: "When did God become important to you?"

APPROPRIATE MOTIVES
FOR BEING A LIFEGUARD

To serve and glorify the Lord.
Colossians 3:23-24

To bear spiritual fruit.
John 15:8

To care for others.
Acts 20:28

To be an example and a model.
1 Peter 5:2-4

To use your God-given gifts.
Ephesians 4:11-13

To spread God's good news.
2 Corinthians 5:19-20

WRONG MOTIVES
FOR BEING A LIFEGUARD

To exalt yourself.
Proverbs 27:2

To feel important or to gain prestige.
1 Thessalonians 2:4-6

Because someone pressured you.
1 Peter 5:2

"I believe it might be accepted as a fairly reliable rule of thumb that the one who is ambitious to lead is disqualified as a leader."

—A. W. Tozer

OVERSEERS RESPONSIBLE

"Now beware! Be sure that you feed and shepherd God's flock—his church, purchased with his blood—for the Holy Spirit is holding you responsible as overseers."

—Acts 20:28

The First Mate

When looking for an apprentice (a future LifeGuard), remember that God is inclined to use the most unlikely people. As Paul said,

> Take a good look, friends, at who you were when you got called into this life. I don't see many of "the brightest and the best" among you, not many influential, not many from high-society families. Isn't it obvious that God deliberately chose men and women that the culture overlooks and exploits and abuses, chose these "nobodies" to expose the hollow pretensions of the "somebodies"? That makes it quite clear that none of you can get by with blowing your own horn before God (1 Corinthians 1:26-29 The Message).

Look for that invisible stamp (see LifeBoat Survival Story: "The Aristotle Stamp" on pages 65-66) on a individual, that imprint God has pressed on a person with leadership potential.

I discovered when working with the youth group at church, that the leaders in the gang were not necessarily the good kids, the model students that did everything right and read their Bibles faithfully. Rather it was the teen who was able to convince the others to sneak out at night during retreats, organized the water balloon battle against the chaperones — the so-called "trouble maker." They were the ones who had the natural leadership abilities. Those are the ones to recruit as youth leaders. (Yeah, I know. It just doesn't seem fair.)

When looking for your First Mate, it may not be the holiest member of your crew. It may be the individual who, in discussions, pushes back the most. The point is, be open. Keep your eyes peeled for the person to whom God leads you.

Once I got a phone call from someone who had just moved to a part of the country I was familiar with. They were

asking I recommend a church there. Each church I recommended, they replied that they had already tried that one, but they didn't like this or that about it. After going through about nine churches, I asked, "Well, tell me about your church back in Ohio. Maybe I can recommend a church like that." They quickly informed me that there was no need doing that because they didn't like that church either.

I couldn't stand it any longer, and my frustration surfaced. "Sounds like you need to start a church," I said irritably. "Obviously you have a better idea of what a church should be like than anyone else. Obviously you could do a better job. I guess God has given you special insight and knowledge on church structure. No doubt about it, you should be a church planter and start your own thing. Maybe you could do it right. Maybe we'd finally end up with a decent church around here." They hung up.

Okay, I overdid it a bit ... well, okay, a lot. What I mean to say is that the logical choice for an apprentice may not be the *best* choice. Pay attention to God's leading.

SPOTTING A FIRST MATE

❖ Pray regularly for new apprentices. Jesus prayed all night before selecting his (Luke 6:12-16). Never neglect the role of spiritual warfare in recruiting apprentice leaders.

❖ Look for those who take assignments seriously.

❖ Look for those who challenge you and even criticize your leadership. They may be potential leaders who are frustrated.

❖ Look for gifted people who you can recognize and affirm.

❖ Look for those who embrace the LifeBoat vision.

CONFIRMING THE FIRST MATE

❖ Share the intent to ask this person to be your First Mate with the Bosun.

❖ You and/or your Bosun should check with others who have ministered with this person or who know this person well. Confirm that they have a teachable spirit and are willing to learn. Ask about potential problems or red flags. Are they servant leaders or leaders who lord it over and abuse their power?

❖ Make sure they meet with your Bosun. It might be a good idea to have a meeting with the pastor, the Bosun, the new First Mate, and you (the LifeGuard). At this meeting, cast the vision of what LifeBoating is all about. Have a prayer of commissioning, during which the three of you pray for this new leader.

DEVELOPING THE FIRST MATE

❖ Work through this book with your First Mate.

❖ Continue to model small group leadership to your First Mate.

❖ Allow your First Mate to lead.

❖ Give regular feedback.

❖ Pray for your First Mate.

❖ Point them toward skill training.

❖ Take your First Mate with you when you are shepherding.

❖ Involve them in meetings with your LifeBoat Bosun.

❖ Help your First Mate find their new apprentice.

The Steward

The basic duties of the Steward are to make sure the crew mates know the where and when of the LifeBoat gatherings and to set the atmosphere. Both of these jobs are critical to the function of the LifeBoat.

There are countless stories about people who were misinformed or missed the details and showed up at the wrong house or on the wrong day. Very frustrating. Especially for new folks who feel uncomfortable anyway. The jitters can spiral and make a shipmate feel like a fool. So making sure the crew knows where and when is hugely important.

Setting the mood is also essential. If the atmosphere is chaotic when people arrive, it will be hard to roll that energy back to a thinking and caring discussion.

The welcome is so crucial. The first greeting and smile do wonders to set the mood. Take time to think through how you can make people feel welcome, comfortable, and glad they came.

THE JOB DESCRIPTION OF THE STEWARD

1. Make sure the crew knows the time and meeting place (reminder calls help).

2. Create a warm, caring atmosphere (lighting, music, etc.).

3. Make sure the arrangements are ready: refreshments, seating, distractions eliminated, child care, etc.

4. Greet people when they arrive.

Steward Tip No. 1
NO PLACE LIKE HOME
Homes are much better meeting sites than church buildings. No matter how hard the designers try to make a room at the church feel homey, a real home wins out every time.

Steward Tip No. 2
SAME TIME, SAME PLACE
It's best to begin a LifeBoat with some consistency. If possible, meet at the same home for the first eight or nine meetings. Same start time and day of the week too.

Once the group is better established, you might want to change things up and rotate houses. It actually helps shipmates

CARE FOR THE FLOCK
"Feed the flock of God; care for it willingly, not grudgingly; not for what you will get out of it but because you are eager to serve the Lord. Don't be tyrants, but lead them by your good example, and when the Head Shepherd comes, your reward will be a never-ending share in his glory and honor."

—1 Peter 5:2-4

to see where their other mates live. When I worked with teens, I found that you could tell a lot about a kid by taking a peek at their room. That's true of a person's house too.

Most kids are eager to show off their rooms (they don't seem to care how messy they are). Adults are a bit different, so be sensitive here. Ask for volunteers. Don't throw out the old last-minute self-invitation — "Hey Joe, we haven't been to your place yet. How about tonight?"

What works best for most LifeBoats is to establish two homes that they switch between. "The Joneses live on the river, so we're at their house when the weather is nice. The Smiths have a big house with lots of space, so when the weather is disagreeable, we're there." Of course, that only works if both the Joneses and the Smiths share the gift of hospitality. Otherwise, it's too much of a burden. Even if you are

HOSPITALITY
"Offer hospitality to one another without grumbling."

—1 Peter 4:9

LIFEBOAT SURVIVAL STORY
"I Want That"

Vienne's husband did not come to church with her. During their decades-long marriage, he had never gone to church with her. In fact, he didn't even believe what she believed. A lover of God and His Word, Vienne steadfastly attended worship and Sunday school and every church Bible study and event we offered.

Vienne invited her husband to come along. He always refused, preferring instead to stay home and watch television.

She prayed for years that her husband would know Jesus, that he would give his heart to Him and be saved. For so long, despite her prayers and her testimony, there was no change.

Then Vienne began to host a LifeBoat in their home. The women met in her living room week after week, deepening their relationships with one another, bonded by their common faith. All the while, her husband sat in his recliner in the den with his TV.

One day Vienne's husband approached me. I was surprised to see him, but nothing shocked me more than what he had come to say to me. He wanted to accept Christ.

I had to ask: "Why?" I wanted to know what did it for him finally, after all these years.

He explained that each week, when Vienne's LifeBoat met at his house, he pretended to be watching television in the next room. Rather than watching his programs, however, he had been paying attention to the LifeBoat. He listened from around the corner, a silent witness to the support and affection the women offered each other.

"I want that," he said with conviction. "I want what they have."

usually at one of the two venues, within the first two years, you ought to hit most of the other homes as well, just to help you get to know each other. You're better able to visualize their life. Be creative. It might be better to meet in Bill's workshop than in his living room.

Steward Tip No. 3
BRING THE TOILET PAPER

If you're not meeting at the Steward's home, make it as easy as you can on the homeowner. Bring the refreshments, paper plates, cups, napkins, and paper towels so all they have to do is open their home. I know one Steward that even brings the toilet paper. Most Stewards of traveling LifeBoats keep a box in the trunk of their car with all the necessary supplies.

Steward Tip No. 4
DRINK IN HAND

Studies show that people feel more comfortable (even protected somehow), if they hold a drink in their hand. So offer your guest a drink to grab onto soon after arriving. The studies go on to say that although people want a drink in their hand when they are standing and talking to others, when they sit down to talk, they want a coaster nearby.

Steward Tip No. 5
NO REFRESHMENT WARS

Avoid the refreshments wars. You know, when it's my turn to provide refreshments, I have to make sure mine are better than your's were last week. These battles can become ridiculous, and they will eventually backfire. People will start backing off the LifeBoat altogether to get out of having to plan appetizers all week.

It's best to set the bar low from the very beginning. "Okay folks, here's the rule: Refreshments will consist of one bag of store-bought cookie (for the junk-food junkies), preferably Chip Ahoy, to keep with our nautical theme; one small platter of fruit or vegetables, preferably carrots and celery (for those who are under the delusion that they are not junk-food junkies); two liters of soda; and coffee. That's it, no more. Well, plus all the tap water you want to drink. But remember, there is a drought going on somewhere in the world."

Scent Stories

A Princeton study concluded that scent memory lasts long than any other. Go ahead, find a Crayola crayon and put it to your nose (it must be Crayola). It immediately takes you back to a time before you had to color within the lines.

Smells also set the mood. Realtors will tell you one of the secrets to selling a house is to bake cookies just before a showing. No need to leave the cookies — you can eat them — the baking aroma does the trick.

Last week I visited a nursing home with the reputation for smelling bad. I dreaded visiting. But when I walked through the front door, all I could smell was fresh-brewed coffee. Wow, what a surprise. I looked around and found that they'd recently moved the coffee bar next to the entrance. Good move.

Dear Steward, when setting the environment for your LifeBoat gathering, pay attention to all the senses, all the potential distractions (Murphy's Law says the phone will always ring when your LifeBoat is having a holy moment), and all welcoming protocols. You are a key participant in creating a LifeBoat that floats.

PASS IT ON

"For you must teach others those things you and many others have heard me speak about. Teach these great truths to trustworthy men who will, in turn, pass them on to others."

—2 Timothy 2:2

The Bosun

The Bosun, short for Boatswain's Mate, is one of the oldest ratings in the U.S. Navy, going back to the American Revolution. In shipping, the bosun trains the crew in maintenance duties, takes charge of damage-control parties, and supervises the loading of cargo, ammunition, fuel, and general stores. They are also integral to the ship's navigation.

In LifeBoat terminology, the Bosun is the person who encourages and supplies up to six LifeBoats. They work mainly with the LifeGuards. They connect with them regularly to see how their LifeBoat is doing, find out if they need anything, hear about the exciting things that are happening, and strategize how to approach the challenges. They resource the LifeGuards by making them aware of small-group materials that might be helpful and making sure the LifeGuard knows what is happening in the church at large.

Just as the LifeGuard acts as a shepherd to his or her crew, so the Bosun shepherds the LifeGuard. Bosuns need to stay apprised of what's going on in the lives of their LifeGuards — their hurts and joys, challenges and accomplishments.

The Bosun will periodically visit their LifeBoats, maybe once a quarter.

But the foremost duty of the Bosun is to hold LifeGuard meetings. LifeBoat leaders cannot flourish in a vacuum. They need to band together periodically with other LifeGuards for encouragement and accountability. The Bosun makes this happen.

Here's how I would approach being a Bosun:

Before a LifeBoat starts, I'd go through this book with the LifeGuard, or see that they get some training. I'd go with them to the training, even if I'd had the training before. This way I'd make sure we were on the same page. As the LifeBoat launches, I'd check in with the LifeGuard every week (assuming it meets weekly) for five or six weeks. Then I would check in every other week for another four weeks, then every three weeks after that. I think once a month is too long a time to go without an evaluation.

I would schedule LifeGuard meetings once every six weeks or so. I'd meet in a restaurant. Feed them dinner. Go around the table and let them tell you how it's going, any tricks to LifeBoating they've learned, any challenges they are facing. I'd leave them with a little skill lesson.

It's important that you honor them at these meetings.

"I'm buying you dinner tonight because you are doing the most important work of the church. You are on the front lines, helping people grow in their walk with God. I know it takes a lot of your time, emotional energy, and spiritual energy. I so appreciate what you are doing."

I bet your church would want to pick up the tab on that dinner for you, Bosun.

GOD'S PEOPLE ARE ABLE

"Why is it that he gives us these special abilities to do certain things best? It is that God's people will be equipped to do better work for him, building up the Church, the body of Christ, to a position of strength and maturity."

—Ephensians 4:12

The Voyage

We've already stressed the importance of regular get-togethers. LifeBoats meet at least twice a month (the minimum requirement). Weekly is preferred. The crews that meet every other week take twice as long to develop, twice as long to build relationships, and twice as long to launch. Everything takes twice as long.

While the main goal of LifeBoats is to spur one another to grow in Christ, each crew will cover these four main areas: Loving/Caring, Bible Study, Prayer/Worship, and Kingdom Work.

The Four Major Components

Loving/Caring

This maybe as simple as inquiring about how everyone is doing. You might ask, "Is there anything we need to pray about in your life this week?" LifeBoats need to strive to meet the individual needs among their crew. A shipmate may be going through a hard time or need advice.

It is often beneficial for a LifeBoat to study relational topics, such as "How to Listen," "How to Build Relationships," or "How to Communicate Needs."

If you are a LifeGuard, you should be able to answer the question, "What's happening in my crew members' lives?"

Here are basic concerns to pay attention to:

❖ Are there unresolved conflicts between members?

❖ Financial needs?

❖ Tough decisions to make?

❖ Health concerns?

❖ Family issues?

And don't forget to celebrate your crew mates' victories, and birthdays, too.

Prayer/Worship
Prayer and worship involves linking our hearts to the heart of God. Effective ministry happens within an atmosphere of prayer, celebration, and worship. Great ministry follows great praying, whether the ministry is to one another or outside our LifeBoat.

It is often beneficial for a LifeBoat to study "The Lord's Prayer," "How to Pray," the "Dynamics of Group Prayer," the "Art of Worship," and so on.

Imagine Jesus sitting in your midst; what would you say to Him?

For other ideas for incorporating prayer and worship, see the chapter titled "The Gathering."

Bible Study
Bible study comprises listening to God and using His Word to confront life's problems. It's not gathering biblical information. Some LifeBoats are privileged to include gifted and qualified Bible teachers, who are mad for deep and detailed teachings. But that is not what a LifeBoat is about, so be careful here. Keep your Bible study devotional and applicable in nature. This is about relationship, not information — relationship with God and relationship with each other.

If Bible knowledge is what you're after, join a class with a qualified teacher (a master teacher situation). If it's important to you to tell someone what you've learned as you've studied late into the night, get a Bible study buddy; or better yet, volunteer to teach a class at church. Too many "Bible Discussion Groups" dissolve into a pool of ignorance.

I may be overstating this, but I've seen too many LifeBoats gravitate to the safe port of Bible study rather than really relating to one another. It seems safer to talk about the first-century customs rather than dealing with the hurts and pains of this week. Bottom line: Your Bible study needs to move as soon as possible to present-day application. Focus on the comfort and direction of the Scriptures, the passages that lead us to trust God, and the verses that call us to follow Him.

Kingdom Work

Relationships are strengthened as you serve the Lord together. LifeBoats may choose to visit shut-ins, take meals to the sick, landscape the church grounds, produce the newsletter, or coordinate the youth ministry. Be sure to pick jobs that you can do together. Tasks that divide the group with each individual working alone do not promote relationships. It is also good to set time limits up front — "We'll do this once a month for six months."

It is true that friends become a force. The Tower of Babel account in Genesis 4 reveals the law of unity, though in a negative way. God said, "Because they are of one mind and one tongue there is nothing they cannot do and there is nothing they will not do." In your LifeBoat, practice unity and working together for positive results.

Captain's Orders

"You can't steer a boat that is not in motion."

Each LifeBoat will cover all four of these areas, but major in one. Most crews will cycle through the four areas, emphasizing one category for several months, and then change their focus to another area.

Some LifeBoats organize around one particular area, and so their identity is tied to that realm. They become known as a Bible study, a prayer group, a service group, or a support group. Even these LifeBoats that major in one area need to cover all four.

PRACTICE FAITH

"So you see, it isn't enough just to have faith. You must also do good to prove that you have it. Faith that doesn't show itself by good works is no faith at all—it is dead and useless."

—James 2:17

Stages of a LifeBoat

In this book, we're shooting for the life-long, close-friends kinds of LifeBoats. Of course, many crews won't last that long, and even those that do change over the course of time.

Take for example Jay and me. We've been LifeBoating together since 1977. We were in grad school when five of us made a little pact that we would push each other to be all that God wanted us to be. The LifeBoat has changed over the years, but Jay and I are the constant. Some have drifted in and some have drifted out. Today our LifeBoat is made up of six guys. The other four have only been with us for six years. Of the original five, one dropped off the map years ago, one I talk to every

---

LIFEBOAT SURVIVAL STORY
"Pool Party"

It was a mission trip, and it was going to be an exciting week for these teenagers. They would be helping a group of blind peers with outdoor activities, such as canoeing, scuba diving, and bicycle riding. One day at the beach. One day at Busch Gardens. At night, there would be campfires and capture-the-flag wars.

All this would be taking place near my old stomping grounds where I used to live, and I wanted to see my old LifeBoat. So I called my friends and told them I wanted to get with them, but that I had eighteen teenagers with me to watch and entertain. Chuck said, "Well, I've got a pool in my backyard. Why don't you bring them over and they can have a pool party while we chat? Just tell me when, and I'll get the old gang together."

It worked brilliantly for a while. The kids were having fun around the pool, and my Life-Boat sat inside, watching through the window and talking up a storm. We started reminiscing about our adventures together. Telling our war stories. Joking and laughing. Having a grand time.

But then the kids started getting bored and cold, and one by one they drifted into the house. They sat quietly on the stairs, on the floor in the corners, around the table in the dining area.

I knew I needed to get them out of there and back to the hotel, but I was having too much fun. The evening wore on and I knew that these bored kids were likely to find some mischief with which to entertain themselves if I didn't change their scenery soon. But I pushed my luck and we stayed late. Finally the conversation slowed, and we headed out.

The next morning we loaded everyone on the bus and headed home. Like any good youth leader, I used the traveling time to debrief. I asked, "So of all the neat things you did this week, what was the best part?" There was a long silence, and then finally one teen answered.

"The best part was sitting around the living room last night listening to you guys tell your stories."

"Really?" I asked, shocked.

And one after another, every kid on that bus agreed that it was the best part of the week.

Here I thought I was boring these young people to tears, but in reality, we were modeling for them what Christian fellowship is all about. They got to see a LifeBoat in action. They got to watch us enjoy one another, rib one another, love one another, and encourage one another.

Now that I think about it, that was the best part.

few years and another I touch base with each year. According to my wife, my face lights up any time the name of one of those original five is mentioned.

A LifeBoat needs new stock every now and then. It infuses fresh energy into the crew. And, of course, there will be a gradual loss as some shipmates move away, die, or lose interest.

Just as an individual goes through the stages of life — child, teen, young adult, mid-life, senior — so will a LifeBoat. The average age of a full-grown boat is about fifty meetings. Of course, every LifeBoat differs, so timeframes are subjective. But the stages of group life seem to be the same.

Formation (first 4-8 meetings).

This first stage is characterized by the feelings of excitement, anticipation, and awkwardness. The crew members collect information about each other. In this stage, the LifeGuard needs to respond by modeling a caring and accepting attitude, promoting (conversational, but meaningful) sharing, and communicating a clear vision. This is a good time for the LifeBoat to study relationships and define goals.

Exploration (spans 8-12 meetings).

Now folks feel more relaxed and comfortable. The LifeBoat will settle into a good Bible study, shipmates will very cautiously try the crew's trust levels with low-risk sharing. The LifeGuard should make moves to generate trust. This is a good time to study the nature of God and create covenants (I will explain covenants later in the following section).

Mid-Life Evaluation (spans 4-8 meetings).

This is a phase when the crew begins to express frustration. Their questions epitomize their doubts: "Are we really open to each other?" and "Will this Life-Boat accomplish anything?" Their feelings will be anxious, impatient, and uncertain. Usually some personality conflicts will surface here. Now is the time for the Life-Guard to move the crew away from self-centeredness and toward Kingdom work. It's an opportune time to study about finding God's will and discovering His plan for your life.

Action (spans 20-40 meetings).

Now the questions advance to express restlessness and energy: "What can we accomplish together?" and "Will we take the risk?" Crew mates will talk about using their gifts. They will take ownership and accept challenges. They'll express feelings of eagerness, but they'll also feel vulnerable. They will openly encourage and support one another. The LifeGuard should provide service opportunities, celebrate results, and begin seeking a *second* First Mate. Study time will be limited, but now is the time to study God's work in the world.

Confidentiality

Safety, Confidentiality, Sensitivity, Forgiveness

For relationships in LifeBoats to be honest and open, there must be an agreement for safety — that what is said in the group will remain confidential, that opinions will be respected, and that differences will be allowed. People must be allowed to fail, and forgiveness must be readily available.

Nothing will kill a group faster than breaking confidentiality (more on this in a later chapter, "How to Sink a LifeBoat").

Your LifeBoat needs to discuss this early on and remind folks of its importance every few months. I've known some Life-Boats to go overboard on this: sweeping the room for bugs before every meeting; posting signs on every door, "Top Secret, Authorized Persons Only"; lowering the "Cone of Silence" before any discussions begin; hiring private detectives to catch loose lips; periodic lie detector tests; and high-level security clearances to join the LifeBoat. Okay, they didn't do all of that, but it sure felt like it.

Common sense is the rule, but converse in detail about what that looks like for your LifeBoat. *Can I tell my spouse when I get home what happened at LifeBoat? What if a shipmate is obviously a danger to themselves or others? Are the jokes top secret too?* Defining what kinds of information need to stay in the room will go a long way to form a protected space to share. Personally, if I have a brilliant idea or say something really witty, I want people to spread the word that I do have some intelligence; but I want my hurts, my failures, and my struggles to be kept confidential within my small circle of true friends.

Setting up some ground rules, or what you might call a LifeBoat covenant, can help crew members understand the importance of keeping things under wraps, as well as adding to their sense of feeling safe to share.

One good idea I've heard is that nothing should be expected to be confidential for the first few months. Then after the crew's gotten to know each other a bit, they will make a covenant about confidentially.

It is a good idea anyway to set up some standards when a LifeBoat is first formed. Some call it a covenant. Some LifeBoats even ask the crew mates to sign the covenant. At the very least, there should be some ground rules, and the LifeBoat ought to review them regularly.

GOSSIP BURNS

"Without wood a fire goes out; without a gossip a quarrel dies down."

—Proverbs 26:20

SAMPLE COVENANT FOR A LIFEBOAT

Priority — While we are part of this LifeBoat, we will give our crew meetings priority.

Participation — Everyone participates and no one dominates.

Confidentiality — Anything personal that is said in our meetings is never repeated outside of the LifeBoat. "Loose lips sink ships."

Respect — Everyone is given the right to their own opinion, and "dumb questions" are encouraged and respected.

Support — Permission is given to call upon each other in time of need, even in the middle of the night.

Courtesy — If you can't make it to the crew meeting, you will call the LifeGuard to let them know you won't be coming.

GOSSIP IS WICKED

"They have become filled with every kind of wickedness, evil, greed and depravity. They are full of envy, murder, strife, deceit and malice. They are gossips, slanderers, God-haters, insolent, arrogant and boastful; they invent ways of doing evil; they disobey their parents; they have no understanding, no fidelity, no love, no mercy."

—Romans 8:29-31

GOSSIP DESTROYS FRIENDSHIP

"A perverse person stirs up conflict, and a gossip separates close friends."

—Proverbs 16:28

Accountability

We'd better take a minute and talk about accountability. It's an important ingredient to growing in Christ, but it can become sick, too.

When I first moved to Louisville, I started visiting churches. One of the first ones I tried gave a good first impression. I met some friendly people before the service, sat with them during the worship, then afterwards asked if anyone wanted to go out for pizza. "That sounds like a plan," someone responded, "just let us check with our 'shepherd' first to see if it's okay with him."

Hmm, I thought suspiciously. I asked a few more questions to feel this out and tried not to look too horrified. What I found out was that every member of this church was assigned a shepherd. It seemed to work pretty well near the top of the pyramid; but in the lower ranks, where fairly new believers acted as shepherds of even newer members, it was pretty bizarre. Shepherds would go over your finances with you, watch over your love life, make relational decisions for you, and so on. It was beyond strange — it was sick.

I finally let them know that I would be happy to join their church if they would make me the pope. They turned me down. And I never did get any pizza.

Accountability can be overbearing, judgmental, and condemning. But the accountability we are talking about in Life-Boats is far from that scenario.

Accountability is voluntary submission to another for support, encouragement, and help in a particular area of your life, giving them some responsibility for assisting you in that area.

Say you're struggling to be romantic with your wife. Somewhere along the line, you stopped wooing her. So at one of your LifeBoat meetings, you ask for help.

Gary responds, "You said you wanted to start preparing meals for her in the evening. I'll tell you what, I'll pray for you every night this week at five o'clock. I'll pray that you can leave the office on time to get to the grocery store."

Mitch even offers to email you some good recipes.

Tori joins in. "If you want, I'll call you on Thursday to see how you're doing with that and remind you to schedule a date night for Friday."

The difference here is that you have asked for help. And they respond by asking you for permission about exactly how to help. Tori will not call you unless you say you'd like that. Either way, you can bet next week someone will ask you how you're doing with the romancing. Somebody will probably also ask Gary if he really prayed for you every evening and Mitch if he emailed recipes.

Accountability is about your LifeBoat crew helping you be more of who you want to be.

LIFEBOAT SURVIVAL STORY
"My Wife Is Out of Town"

My men's LifeBoat had been meeting for about two years and we'd grown pretty close. One night, Greg, one of the members of the crew, called to say, "Man, am I in trouble. My wife has taken the kids and gone to visit her parents in Arkansas for two weeks. There's this girl at work who's let me know that I can have her if I want her. I don't know what I'm going to do. Temptation is mounting, I can't get her off my mind, and I've got two weeks to go."

Well I told him what any good Christian would say — "I'll pray for you" — and got off the phone. But then I called a few of the guys in the LifeBoat, and for the next two weeks, Greg had breakfast with one of us, lunch with another, and dinner with a third. And then, every night after nine o'clock, I gave him a call and asked, "What're you doing, man?"

LifeBoats can save your life.

CASTING THE VISION
"Not Enough Lifeboats: The Titanic Tragedy"

If it is true that the best way to disciple believers is through LifeBoats ... and if it is true that the best way for believers to get the spiritual comfort they need in times of crisis is through a LifeBoat ... and if it is true that all people long for close relationships that they can rely on like a LifeBoat provides ... then why do large numbers of Christians not have a LifeBoat?

Good question. The *Titanic* was equipped with too few lifeboats and only a number of those were launched filled to capacity. Why?

Read the following article from HistoryOnTheNet.com:

One of the factors that makes the sinking of the *Titanic* so memorable is the fact that lives were needlessly lost. There were not enough lifeboats on board to hold all the passengers and crew and when the lifeboats were launched they were not filled to capacity.

The information on this page represents some of the main facts relating to the lifeboats on board *Titanic*.

At the British Inquiry into the *Titanic* disaster, Sir Alfred Chalmers of the Board of Trade was asked why regulations governing the number of lifeboats required on passenger ships had not been updated since 1896. Sir Alfred gave a number of reasons for this (question 22875):

(continued)

- Due to advancements that had been made in ship building it was not necessary for boats to carry more lifeboats.
- The latest boats were stronger than ever and had watertight compartments making them unlikely to require lifeboats at all.
- Sea routes used were well-travelled meaning that the likelihood of a collision was minimal.
- The latest boats were fitted with wireless technology.
- That it would be impossible for crew members to be able to load more than sixteen boats in the event of a disaster.
- That the provision of lifeboats should be a matter for the ship owners to consider.

Sir Alfred also stated that he felt that if there had been fewer lifeboats on *Titanic*, then more people would have been saved. He believed that if there had been fewer lifeboats then more people would have rushed to the boats and they would have been filled to capacity, thus saving more people. (questions 22960/1)

Titanic carried 20 lifeboats, enough for 1,178 people. The existing Board of Trade required a passenger ship to provide lifeboat capacity for 1,060 people. *Titanic's* lifeboats were situated on the top deck. The boat was designed to carry 32 lifeboats, but this number was reduced to 20 because it was felt that the deck would be too cluttered.

At the British investigation, Charles Lightoller as the senior surviving officer was questioned about the fact that the lifeboats were not filled to capacity. They had been tested in Belfast on 25 March 1912 and each boat had carried 70 men safely. When questioned about the filling of lifeboat number six, Lightoller testified that the boat was filled with as many people as he considered to be safe. Lightoller believed that it would be

impossible to fill the boats to capacity before lowering them to sea without the mechanism that held them collapsing. He was questioned as to whether he had arranged for more people to be put into the boats once it was afloat. Lightoller admitted that he should have made some arrangement for the boats to be filled once they were afloat. When asked if the crew member in charge of lifeboat number six was told to return to pick up survivors, the inquiry was told that the crew member was told to stay close to the ship (questions 13883 - 13910). Lifeboat number 6 was designed to hold 65 people. It left with 40.

Titanic also carried 3,500 lifebelts and 48 life rings — useless in the icy water. The majority of passengers that went into the sea did not drown, but froze to death.

Many people were confused about where they should go after the order to launch the lifeboats had been given. There should have been a lifeboat drill on 14 April, but the Captain cancelled it to allow people to go to church.

Many people believed that *Titanic* was not actually sinking but that the call to the lifeboats was actually a drill and stayed inside rather than venture out onto the freezing deck. ❖

LIFEBOAT SURVIVAL STORY
"Alone at Sea"

It was the fourth time Rob had called me in five days. He was beside himself. He had structured his entire life — heart and soul — around his wife. She was his whole support system. Now, apparently she was tired of that role, and she had left him for the nice, capable fellow down the street.

I had not heard from Rob in over ten years. I lived on the East Coast of the Mainland and he had moved to an island in Hawaii. That's 4,835 miles between us!

He didn't know what to do or where to turn. Every suggestion I gave him, he had ten reasons why that wouldn't work.

"You've lived there for years," I said, "surely by now you've developed a band of believers. Surely you've surrounded yourself with friends that know the situation much better than I. I think they can serve you better than I can."

But no, he hadn't established any meaningful relationships. It was just him and his wife ... or it had been the two of them. Now she had jumped ship. They had attended a church, but they hadn't really gotten to know anyone, much less form a LifeBoat.

"Who are your closest friends?" I asked.

"She is. She was it."

I was so frustrated I could have screamed. From his Facebook posts, I could see that he'd found time to surf, hike, and see all the latest movies and reality shows. He had gotten around to doing everything except a LifeBoat. And now, without a life preserver, he was alone at sea and drowning in panic.

How many times have I seen this? People run to a pastor or a counselor (people who hardly know them) expecting them to be able to comfort or advise them. Here they are seeking help in making important life-changing decisions from mere acquaintances or even strangers. They stand at a major crossroads or a point of grief, the roof has caved in, and they are alone at sea with no LifeBoat in sight.

"Rob, this aloneness is what God wanted to spare you from when he designed Life-Boats."

An iceberg had struck his ship and he was going down fast, without a LifeBoat. Had they taken the time to commit to a crew — dare I say — he might have been clued in to what he wasn't providing his wife, or she might have recognized what she was lacking.

I beg you: Build your LifeBoat and fill that vessel to capacity *before* you run into the thing that will sink you.

Captain's Orders

"Even those who swim the English Channel alone want a lifeboat close by."

The Gathering

I know I've said it before, and I hate to sound like a broken record, but the more often your LifeBoat meets, the faster the relationships develop and the sooner you'll cross that magical threshold where the bonds are tight enough that real life change can occur. After you reach that point, your LifeBoat may be able to get away with lengthening the time between meetings.

The LifeBoat I've been in the longest meets quarterly; but when we get together, it's a two-day gathering — an overnighter. And we also touch base with each other over the phone and via email. We only use email for updates; serious conversations

happen on the phone or, even better, over lunch. That works best for us because we live all over the state. The point I'm trying to make is that relationships take time.

If at all possible, hold your meetings in a home. This is preferable. More real relating seems to happen around the coffee table in the living room than in a sterile church classroom. If the LifeBoat crew is less than six, a restaurant might be appropriate — but not Chuck E. Cheese's or a sports bar with a hundred TVs. Something a bit quieter with less distractions is fine.

Child care for those LifeBoats with young parents is frequently a challenge. I know several churches that pay for regular nannies. Some parents choose to leave their kids at home with a babysitter. Others bring their kids to the LifeBoat, where a sitter watches all the children collectively. Either way, if paid child care is used, the church picks up the tab.

One pastor remarked that LifeBoats were a major focus of his church, but the church budget didn't exactly reflect that.

"LifeBoats are fairly inexpensive. How can our budget better reflect our emphasis on LifeBoats?"

I'm so glad you asked! Paying for child care speaks volumes, saying that kids are important to the church, as well as LifeBoats and families. Besides, most young couples can't afford child care.

Some LifeBoats that are made up entirely of parents prefer to bring their kids in the LifeBoat. What usually works is to include the kids in the meeting for the prayer and worship time, let them watch a movie or play in a separate room during the discussion, and then bring them back for the refreshments. I've known four couples — all parents — who have two LifeBoats: one for the husbands and one for the wives, and they alternate weeks, so that one parent is home with the children on Monday nights while the other is with his or her LifeBoat.

Now let's take a look at the different parts of a LifeBoat meeting.

Preparation

Be prepared for your LifeBoat's gathering by making a plan. Ask yourself, *What is my desired outcome for this meeting?*

I want my crew mates to *know*

_____.

I want my crew mates to *feel*

_____.

I want my crew mates to *do*

_____.

I want my crew mates to *plan*

_____.

Arrange for different crew members to use their various gifts to serve the LifeBoat in diverse ways. Crew mates can participate by guiding discussions, preparing social activities, leading prayer time, making phone calls, tracking service opportunities in the church, organizing group outreach, hosting the LifeBoat, becoming a First Mate, conducting worship, writing notes and cards, visiting shipmates in need, maintaining calendars and schedules, keeping track of birthdays, choosing curriculum, or providing feedback.

Openers
Icebreakers allow people to get used to talking and sharing with a group in relaxed conditions. When a LifeBoat first launches,

the questions ought to remain casual and non-invasive (Where did you grow up? What school did you attend? How did you come to church? Where do you work?). This allows the shipmates to tell their stories.

As the LifeBoat grows comfortable with each other, more in-depth questions are appropriate. Opening questions should be designed to elicit more than simple yes-and-no answers.

What's your favorite movie and why?

If you won a trip to anywhere in the world for a week, where would you go and why?

Outside your family, who is your number-one advisor in life?

If you were part of the landscape today, what would you be? (The mud on the bottom of the lake, the crescent moon, etc.)

What is your biggest pet peeve?

People might be surprised to find out that I _____.

A billionaire offers to buy you three wishes. What would you wish for?

If you went blind today, what would you miss seeing the most?

What's the most daring thing you've ever done?

You have one minute to address the nation. What would you say?

Describe the circumstances of your first kiss.

If you could perform one miracle, what would you do?

What's the biggest lie you ever told?

If given a choice, how would you want to die?

If you could go to college again, what would you study?

What's the worst storm or disaster you've been through?

Describe the most boring day you remember.

If you were a time traveler, what time would you like to visit and why?

Not counting God or your family, who is your best friend?

What's the greatest adventure you've ever taken?

How are you most like your parents?

What do you wish someone had told you before you got married?

I'm all thumbs or a bundle of nerves when it comes to _____.

What are some things you remember about your grandparents?

What does your name mean and why were you named that?

What is your most memorable dream?

If you had to eat a crayon, what color would you choose and why?

What was the best gift you ever received as a child?

If you could raise one person from the dead, who would you choose and why?

Who was one of the most interesting people that you and your family ever entertained?

What's the nicest thing anyone has ever said about you?

What one thing would you like your obituary to say about you?

What is your favorite city and why?

Where do you go and what do you do when life gets too much for you?

Who was the neighborhood bully where you grew up, and why was s/he so scary?

If your house was on fire, what three items would you try to save?

What was your first job, and what do you remember most about it?

Who was the best boss you ever had? Why?

Who was your hero when you were growing up?

What do you think people say about you behind your back?

Tell us about your wedding day? (Bring photographs.)

Why do you sin? (No simplistic answers please.)

When was the last time you cried?

When was the last time you laughed so hard it hurt?

In what area of your life would you like to have more peace?

If you were one day to have a worldwide reputation for something, in what area would you like that to be?

Describe a grade-school teacher that made a big impression on you.

If you were given a year's sabbatical but couldn't travel more than 150 miles from home, what would you do?

What's the most useless thing in your house, and why do you still have it?

In general, people worry too much about _____.

An emotion I often feel but don't express is _____.

Why are you glad God made the person to your right?

What do you look forward to as you grow older?

Prayer & Worship

As we discussed in an earlier chapter, a worshipful atmosphere is key. Here are some ideas to incorporate prayer and worship in your crew meeting.

Singing: If a shipmate plays piano or guitar or sings, ask him or her to lead the group in a chorus, hymn, or praise song.

Song Share: You might ask each crew member to share their favorite worship song; they can read the lyrics aloud as a prayer, or mediate a discussion around that song, including why it's meaningful.

Eucharist: You may take communion with your LifeBoat to remember the sacrifice God made, giving his Son for our sins. Bread and wine not necessary — you can use milk and cookies if you want.

Worship: Crew members can come together and conduct a short version of a church worship service (15-20 minutes), with music, video, readings, and Scripture.

Prayer: Spoken prayer — even in intimate gatherings — can be uncomfortable for those who are not used to it. A good way to introduce corporate prayer in your LifeBoat would be to try sentence prayers, asking each shipmate to speak (pray) a brief sentence. When it's appropriate, laying on of hands is a powerful way to pray for members of the crew. Be sure your shipmates are fine to pray aloud before you put them on the spot.

Discussion: Talk about worship — what it means to each crew mate, and what it means to God.

Testimonies

Why not ask a member of your crew to give their testimony at your next gathering? It could be the story of how they came to know Christ. Or it can be something more recent, like an answer to prayer or how God helped them through a tough time.

Verbalizing our experience with God helps us think through what our faith is all about — so it strengthens the faith of the person giving the testimony. As they share their feelings, it also makes them feel more connected with their crew.

Testimonies will make your LifeBoat more personal. I'd suggest having someone give a testimony every fourth meeting. Give everyone, except the most introverted, a chance to share their story.

Discussion

The key to good group discussion is to ask the right questions.

Start with a short, creative illustration or story that explains why you want to discuss this topic. Introduce the topic, and then follow up with the right questions.

Launching Questions

These are typically designed to answer the questions, *What do I know? What do I feel? What should I do?*

—"What do we learn about friendship from Job's friends as he faced his problems?"

—"What is it that often drives us to fear intimacy with one another?"

—"What can we do as a LifeBoat to diminish this fear?"

—"What do you think was going through Elihu's (Job's friend's) mind at that time?"

—"Is our LifeBoat stuck in this kind of relating? What steps can we take to develop a greater forgiveness factor in our boat?"

— "Would you be tempted in this situation?"

— "What three commandments do we find in this passage?"

Responding Questions

Once your crew is talking, you need to respond in a way that keeps it going. Try rephrasing the question.

— "You seem to be asking, 'How can we develop trust in our group?' "

Personalizing Questions

Make the story/topic personal.

— "How would you respond if Jesus were to ask you that?"

Ask for consensus.

— "Are we saying that everyone must obey this command?"

Summarizing Questions

— "That's a great response. Are there other comments as well?"

— "So what we see in this passage is...?"

Applying Questions

Make the story/topic applicable.

— "What difference does this make for you and me?"

— "What will you do this week as a result of our discussion?"

Be prepared to respond, as the crew responds.

Appropriate Response

When a crew mate shares a hurt, we must respond appropriately.

— "That must have been painful for you to share. It makes me sad just hearing about it."

— "That was a traumatic childhood experience. How did you deal with it then? How do you deal with it now?"

Affirming Response

— "That's a terrific insight. How did you come to that realization?"

— "What a great victory. How has that impacted your relationship with your husband?"

Participatory Response

Involve the other shipmates in response.

— "Has anyone else in the group been in a similar circumstance? How did you deal with it?"

Vision Casting

As a LifeBoat LifeGuard, you'll find yourself doing a lot of vision casting. While on the phone recruiting LifeBoat crew mates... As you launch your first gathering... When you need to remind a shipmate what the LifeBoat is all about...

In fact, you'll do a bit of vision casting at every meeting (usually at the end).

But at certain key moments during your LifeBoat's voyage, you'll spend the bulk of the time casting the vision.

Vision casting is an ability that separates a valuable LifeGuard from an ineffective leader. It's what keeps the LifeBoat focused and on course. Casting a vision is painting a picture of the preferred future — an exhibit of sorts. This picture of the future should be inspiring, compelling, and something your LifeBoat can rally around. It needs to be visual. Think of yourself as an artist painting a word picture of what the future looks like. A proper vision statement is concise, clear, convincing and easily communicated.

As a LifeGuard, you know what you want your LifeBoat to look like in the future. Your motive is to make that vision a reality as soon as possible.

A quality vision allows you to say no to certain things. But a quality vision is also one that others can plug their vision into. It's all-inclusive and unifying. Therefore, it is crucial that you work together with your crew members to develop a vision. You may even decide to create a vision statement. With no vision, your LifeBoat will drift aimlessly. ("Without a vision, the people will perish.")

In forming your vision, remember these areas:

Maturing Spiritually

Growing Relationally

Fostering Safety

Generating Excitement

Welcoming Outsiders

After picturing what you want your LifeBoat to look like in each of these areas, jot down some action steps and target dates for completing those steps.

Throughout this book you will see "Vision Casting" boxes that we hope will help you cast a vision of what your LifeBoat could be. Even if you're leading a Church LifeBoat, cast the vision of a Lifelong LifeBoat. Also the "LifeBoat Survival Stories" scattered throughout this book will help you cast vision. Those stories may also help you remember stories of your own that illustrate what a LifeBoat can be.

LIFEBOAT SURVIVAL STORY
"The Aristotle Stamp"

My son, Pepper, was a student at George Washington University in the nation's capital. While riding the Metro one day, a man spoke to him.

"Are you in the Navy, young man?" he asked.

When Pepper confirmed that he was in the Navy ROTC at GWU, the man replied, "I can always tell a shipmate when I see one!"

This was Chief Robinson, who was visiting the city with his wife to check out the university for their nephew, who would be attending. They invited Pepper to dinner that evening.

Later I received a phone call from the chief, after Pepper accepted the offer to vacation with Chief and Mrs. Robinson and their nephew in Quebec. He said he knew I must be concerned that my son would be leaving the country with a strange couple that we didn't know. He explained what the young men would be doing and sent me the agenda, which was detailed in such a way as only a United States Navy chief petty officer could organize.

During that trip, the chief coached Pepper in Navy protocol and social behaviors, teaching him to answer "yes sir" and to always wear a collared shirt to a meal. They dined in restaurants with a dress code, requiring Pepper to wear a jacket and tie. The chief taught my son how to drink and smoke cigars (something he wouldn't learn from his Baptist preacher father) and to quit responsibly at a reasonable amount.

Chief Robinson continued to mentor Pepper over the years, and to this day, he looks after my son.

Around the same time, Pepper ran into a Marine Corps major on campus who needed a pull-ups companion. Three times a week, they headed to the pull-ups bars and tried to out-do one another.

Major Richardson—and the chief as well—instilled an enthusiasm about the military in my son. Both men related their war stories, always putting a positive but realistic perspective on it and ending ultimately with an "I-lived-to-tell-about-it" attitude.

One day I went sailing with Pepper and Major Richardson. When Pepper left us to head into the cabin and I was alone on deck with the major, I asked him, "So, there are two of you now who have taken my son under your wing. Is this something the military tells you to do? Because I'm grateful to you both, but I don't understand..."

He paused and took a serious drag on his cigar. "Two things, Revered Ailor. One, I love the Corps. And two, I'm not the future."

"But why Pepper?" I persisted.

"Like Aristotle spoke about the stamp on a person's soul ... I look for the stamp."

In essence, he was telling me that when he looked at my son, he saw the stamp of leadership. He saw a young man who would carry on the substance of the Corps that he loved.

(continued)

65

LIFEBOAT SURVIVAL STORY *continued*

This experience makes me think about discipleship and what this would mean.

Two things. One, I love the Church. And two, I'm not the future.

This is a standpoint we must take in our churches. If we love the Church, we will find others to mentor, to take under our wings (to disciple).

The same is true of LifeBoats. Teach LifeBoating to others to ensure the future of these relationships. Look for the Aristotle Stamp in others. When you see it, invite that potential shipmate to see the insides of your LifeBoat—the mechanics of the operation—the heart of the organism. Let them learn the ropes. Instill in them an enthusiasm for LifeBoats and Christian relationships, and the Church will endure.

"It is by means of small-boat sailing
that the real sailor is best schooled."

—*Jack London*

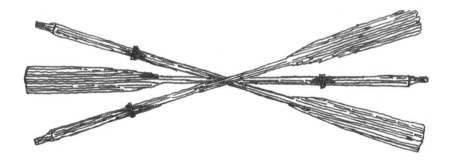

66

Picking the Crew

Our next-door neighbors were nice folks. Generous and friendly. They wanted to be neighborly and we wanted to be neighborly ... but they seemed to vibrate on a different frequency and we just didn't connect. Our lots were small in the neighborhood, so we slept less than thirty feet from each other. Thankfully there were several walls between us. Nevertheless, we did make a point to get together periodically. Just to be neighborly. I found myself praying on the short walk from our front door to theirs, "Lord, please help us to be on the same wavelength as our neighbors tonight." Then I revised that prayer. "No, no, on second thought, put them on *our* wavelength. I don't want to be on theirs."

I'm certain there are people in your life like that. There's nothing really wrong with them. You can't put your finger on exactly what it is, but your personality and theirs just don't mix. So let's bust the myth right now that any random group of Christians can LifeBoat together. It's not quite that simple. You cannot LifeBoat with just anyone. Just because you can all meet on Tuesday night, or because you live in the same neighborhood, does not mean you are compatible as a LifeBoat.

Initiate a culture in your church that makes it acceptable to try out different LifeBoats. In fact, I'd say the cause of most small-group ministry failures is because the church made it nearly impossible to switch groups ... or at least awkward to do so. Make it perfectly clear that it's expected for folks to sample different LifeBoats. More often than not, people have to move through several before they find the crew that clicks.

Hopefully, this chapter will save you a lot of headaches, embarrassment, and edgy moments. How do you pick your Lifeboat crew? How do you choose the people that you'll be doing life with? How do you identify those with whom you'll be

---

PRAY BEFORE YOU PICK

"One day soon afterwards he went out into the mountains to pray, and prayed all night. At daybreak he called together his followers and chose twelve of them to be the inner circle of his disciples. (They were appointed as his 'apostles,' or 'missionaries.') Here are their names: Simon (he also called him Peter), Andrew (Simon's brother), James, John, Philip, Bartholomew, Matthew, Thomas, James (the son of Alphaeus), Simon (a member of the Zealots, a subversive political party), Judas (son of James), Judas Iscariot (who later betrayed him)."

—Luke 6:12-16

able to share secrets, struggles, and inspiration?

Jesus didn't gamble when He chose His disciples. He didn't draw a line in the sand and say, "Whoever is available and willing, come on over." He handpicked His LifeBoat. Luke 6 makes a point of saying that Jesus prayed all night before choosing his Twelve. Should we do any less?

There are five criteria to consider when you pick your crew (Bill Hybels lists four. I've added a fifth: The Trust Factor):

The Affinity Factor
The Trust Factor
The Intensity Factor
The Availability Factor
The Stability Factor

Occasionally the church might sponsor a "Fishing Pond Event," where you can go and meet the LifeGuards of different boats, see when theirs meets, and chat with some other folks who are looking for a LifeBoat. If you let the church know that you're interested in exploring LifeBoats, they will probably suggest two or three to try out. But as you explore, keep these five criteria in mind.

The Affinity Factor

Affinity is a feeling. You may not be close to the same age, or IQ, or socio-economic background, but you really like each other. You connect easily. They are interesting and easy to get along with. You click. You mesh. You vibrate on the same frequency. You feel an affinity with them.

Dave and I are as different as night and day. He's blue collar; I'm white collar. I want to get things right; he just wants to get it done. He and I have made lots of road trips together, usually to faraway funerals we needed to attend. Or maybe I should say, *I* needed to attend. I resist such obligations and Dave knows it, so he calls and pushes me. "So-and-so's mother died, and we need to drive out there. When do you want to leave?" Now that Dave is going, I find myself wanting to take that trip I was dreading.

He is the best traveling companion. Our relationship is easygoing — minimal friction, maximum affinity. The conversation never stops. We joke, get serious, tell stories. He can say the most outlandish things, and I just laugh. I love hearing about his world. It is so different from mine. I want to pick up his attitude toward life. He helps me to not take myself so seriously. We've learned to overlook each other's quirks. We look forward to being with one another. Like I said — positive affinity.

The bottom line on the affinity factor is that you're going to be spending a lot of time with these people you LifeBoat with. You'd better like them.

The Trust Factor

Can we trust you?

Our LifeBoat had been meeting for two years. We were comfortable with each other. Sharing was open and honest. We'd gotten past the putting on airs for each other. We'd removed our masks. I felt a freedom with my shipmates. This meeting, however, was going to be different ... but I hadn't yet noticed. Or rather, the difference didn't register until it was too late.

A new fellow was attending the Life-Boat. I didn't know him, but some of the others did, and together we'd decided to

give him a try. Actually, we were thinking, we'd let him give *us* a try. But again, this had not registered with me.

Our LifeGuard opened the floor with the simplest of questions: "So, what's new?" I was reeling from a distressing family matter, so I launched right in. I explained that our son's wife of six short months, whom we'd all fallen in love with, had dropped a bomb. Out of the blue she announced she wanted out of the marriage immediately and she moved out. I continued to explain the situation in full: the girl, the boy, my wife's reaction, and my feelings the best I could... I was still in shock.

One by one the LifeBoat expressed their dismay. They'd listened to me for the last three years say how delighted we were by my son's blossoming relationship and the fairy-tale wedding that followed.

But then the new guy spoke up. "Why didn't you insist that they take premarital counseling before the wedding?"

This was trailed by other accusatory questions. Then he shook his head in astonishment that I hadn't had the sense to foresee all this and intervene. He didn't say it outright, but I got the distinct impression that he thought I was a lousy father.

I was feeling pretty low when I entered the meeting, but I was dragging when I left. I felt betrayed. Fortunately, he never came back. He was

LIFEBOAT SURVIVAL STORY
"How Can You Be Depressed?"

It was a hard year for me —1982— and I still don't know why. I had a good job, good family, no outstanding crisis to speak of, but nonetheless, I felt depressed. I was walking around with my chin dragging the ground.

My LifeBoat was concerned and decided I needed help. But in their opinion any old help wasn't appropriate for one of their LifeBoat mates. So they jumped through all kinds of hoops to get me an appointment with one of the most famous Christian psychiatrists in the world, James Dobson. He was speaking at a huge rally on the Washington Mall, which meant he was going to be on our side of the country that day. All four of my LifeBoat friends drove me to D.C. As Dr. Dobson came off the stage after his speech, there I stood at the bottom of the steps with two of my friends. They introduced me, then Dobson and I walked a few blocks together to a car. We got into the backseat and continued our chat, while a driver steered the car through the streets. Then finally the car pulled over somewhere in city, and the driver said, "This is where you get out." I climbed out of the backseat, still thinking how surreal it all was.

I took me a minute to realize that I didn't know where I was or how I was going to get home. I looked around, stunned, and there, leaning against a wall, was one of my crew mates, smiling ear to ear.

I don't remember much about the conversation I had with the famous man. Although I'm sure he gave me some helpful advice, the only thing I remember, after he asked how tall I was, is that he suggested I play basketball at least three times a week. The exercise would do me good, he said. Dr. Dobson loved playing basketball.

The depression left me soon after that. But I don't think it was the b-ball. I was dumb-founded and moved by how much trouble my LifeBoat had gone through to get me some help. You know when people care for you that much, you can't stay depressed for long.

---

probably too self-righteous to meet with a bunch of deadbeat dads like us.

Trust is more than keeping confidence. Trust is knowing that your LifeBoat will rightly respond to what you share. If you're going to open the closet doors of your life to others, you need to trust them with what's inside.

When a LifeBoat first forms, the trust levels will be slight. People will start to feel each other out. One shipmate will launch a subtle "trust missile" into the LifeBoat to see how people will respond. As time goes on, the sharing will deepen. The trust levels will swell.

I'm happy to report that in all my years of LifeBoating, the attitude of the new guy I just described is rare. Most people are not that judgmental. Most believers are believers because they are aware of their own desperate need for a Savior. Most Christians understand that we are all sinners trying to make it in a thorny world.

How many times have I seen that missile launched? A crew member ventures out and shares a dark or private part of

who is more conscious of the log in their own eye than the speck in their brother's eye.

It's too bad you can't directly ask, "Can we trust you?" at the launch of a LifeBoat. That would be like asking a liar, "Are you lying?" Any accomplished liar would answer with a quick, "No, I never lie." Feeling out the trust factor in people takes some time, but it's certainly worth the effort.

The Intensity Factor

A sport can be fun ... or it can be misery ... especially when it's a non-professional, no-money-involved sport. Of course, it's more likely to be fun if you win. But what are the other factors that determine fun sports from miserable sports? One element is fairly predictable. It's the intensity of the other players on the team. You put highly competitive people on the same team with people who are merely looking for some amusement and the frustration begins.

We used to play Wallyball with our church (it's basically volleyball played on a handball court). It was a pickup game every Thursday night at the YMCA. Most nights, it was entertaining. But other nights, the mood moved to total frustration, because a couple of the folks who showed up to play were all in. In their opinion, you had to dive for every shot. If you were not bleeding, you were not trying. They expected total sacrifice on every play. Others on the team were there strictly for fun and recreation. "Oops, I missed!" was followed by giggles. "Can I have a do-

themselves expecting a judgmental reaction, only to be amazed that their LifeBoat surrounded them with love, understanding, and empathy.

I talked to a man last month who was truly awestruck by the way his LifeBoat responded to each other.

"In our LifeBoat, most of the troubles we have, we've brought on ourselves. Yet there is no judgment, no beating each other up. In Jesus Christ, there really isn't any condemnation." (He was referring to Romans 8:1.)

A fitting way to define a Pharisee is someone who likes rules — particularly one who likes to make up rules as they go along and who is looking to catch someone doing something wrong. We're all Pharisees to one degree or another; but when picking your crew, try to avoid these self-proclaimed experts. Go for the individual over?"

"No," a competitor would spout, "the rules are very clear." Then they'd quote the directive from memory, including page number, section, and point.

"Oh, come on! It's just a game."

The game turned to woe for both the dedicated and the giggler. The problem was the difference in the level of intensity by which they approached the game.

When looking for your crew mates, be sure to consider the intensity level. Some people are so intense, they will want to get straight into the operating room in the first meeting. "Okay, that was an interesting icebreaker, but when are we going to take the gloves off? When are we going to re-ally start working on each other? I want to straighten out some issues." While others are thinking, "Man, I hope we never get to *that* point."

Fortunately, most people are balanced, somewhere in the middle of the road. But take care to consider where you are on the scale, and join a crew that is close to you in intensity. Sure, you'll want a couple shipmates who are more intense to pull the LifeBoat along, and you'll want others who are more laid back to keep the fun factor alive in your crew. But too wide of a swing will ruin it for everyone.

The Availability Factor

Last week, I drove back from Richmond (ninety minutes) to be at my LifeBoat gathering. Why? Because it's a priority for me. I know that I need to have a certain level of commitment for this thing to float. I also know that my fellow crew mates need to make it a priority as well.

LifeBoats take time. Most people I know don't have three hours a week of time unspoken for. They are going to have to carve out the time if they want their LifeBoat to remain buoyant.

As you explore who to LifeBoat with, one red flag to look out for is this stance: "I'll make it when I can." Is it or is it not a priority for you?

There have been times when my life has become so full that I begin to see new friends as another time consumer. That is not a good frame of mind to be in. It is a warning that I am in desperate need of balance in my life.

Making time for a LifeBoat is not pain-less. You have to make the time, reshuffle schedules and commitments. You may need to change league nights. Be willing to drive thirty minutes.

Being available is your responsibility.

The Stability Factor

Now here's a delicate topic, but it really needs to be stated. Some would be bet-ter served by first working out some of their personal struggles with a professional counselor or therapist. Most LifeBoats are not prepared, equipped, or designed to do therapy. So when picking your crew, you need to look for a certain level of emotion-al health or psychological stability.

Some people are carrying around unfinished business with their parents or other authority figure. Some are dealing with a past trauma or disappointment. What often happens is the LifeBoat begins to center on that issue, and the crew members become amateur therapists, which doesn't serve anyone.

LifeBoats are brilliant at helping its shipmates navigate rough spots, points of grief or struggle, even personal crisis and heartbreak. But critical need demands more than a LifeBoat can provide.

We are talking about people who are stuck. One way to recognize this condition is when, no matter what the topic, it comes back to the same hangup every time. It's like they push play on their tape, retelling the story of their hurt. But while you're making suggestions or addressing their situation, they are rewinding the tape. And when it's their turn to respond, they play the tape again. They're stuck on repeat.

Your church can probably suggest some excellent pastoral counselors that can help, but pyschoanalysis is not what Life-Boats are designed for.

LifeBoats can, however, help you stay unstuck from issues you used to be stuck on. (For more on this, please refer to "Extra Grace Required" on pages 96-97.)

"The little boat you are in, and know in every plank, and love too, becomes more than ever a cherished friend."
—John MacGregor

CASTING THE VISION
"Through the Roof"

My friend George, whom I have LifeBoated with for over thirty years, says, "Everyone needs four friends." He is referring to the gospel story in Matthew 9, Mark 2 and Luke 5, in which the friends of a paralyzed man tear a hole in the roof of a crowded house and lower the man to Jesus' feet. The man is healed because of his friends' faith. "You need four friends, one for each corner of your mat. Friends who will do whatever it takes to get you to Jesus." George has got a good grip on one corner of my mat. And I strive to keep a firm grasp on his mat as well.

LIFEBOAT SURVIVAL STORY
"You Have What It Takes"

Don had been doing the hard stuff at work, dealing with the things no one else wanted to. It was up to him to make the hard calls that other people should have made years ago. Everyone knew that those two employees were no good for the company. Their attitudes and subpar performance were dragging everyone down and disrupting the success of the business. They weren't bad people — quite nice actually — but not cut out for this industry.

Don had tried all kinds of tricks to get them on board, but it just wasn't going to work out. Finally he made a tough choice and took the actions necessary to remove them from the organization. He knew the pain for the employees and the company would be temporary, but the future in the long term would be better for both.

Now he was getting backlash and lots of it. These two had made friends at work, and those friends were upset. Although no one was saying they'd been valuable workers or that the company would suffer without them, the other employees were hurt about their friends "being treated that way." One man had said what others were thinking: "It probably had to be done, I just think the way it was done was wrong."

Don had been reviewing his actions and motives with our LifeBoat over the many months this situation had been going on. Now, he and his wife and I were standing in a hallway at a convention, and he was telling me the latest — the accusations and attacks on his character and motives. Don had become the bad guy. He was really second-guessing himself.

I interrupted him. "Don, let me tell you a little secret. It's *never* done the right way, because there is no good way to do it. That's always the accusation. You're young and you've never done this before, but let me assure you that you've handled it in the best way possible. Every step of the way you've considered your employees — both the ones that are leaving and the ones that are staying — as well as your customers. Listen, the majority of people in business would have taken the easy way out — the path of least resistance — but you stepped up to the plate. Yes, there will be plenty of ugliness for a while, but then it will settle down. Within a couple of months, attitudes will change, the atmosphere at work will lighten, and the company will move forward faster. It's hard to see it now, but the future is bright. And as for those employees... Within a year, they'll have other jobs that they like better and that suit them better.

"Listen Don, I know you. I know what you're capable of and I know your heart. I've watched you for years. You can do this. You have what it takes."

Suddenly, his wife stepped forward and hugged me. It took me by surprise. I wasn't expecting that reaction at all. She held me for what seemed like a long time. "Oh, thank you, thank you! That is just what we needed to hear. Thank you..."

I thought I was giving Don a reality check. I hadn't realized that his wife needed the encouragement as well. Because we had LifeBoated together, Don knew that I would be honest with him and not merely tell him what he wanted to hear. Encouragement from a respected LifeBoat crew bolsters confidence and relieves doubts.

Boating Skills

Intimacy Skills

Being Real Through Transparency & Vulnerability

I once met a military leader who said, "A leader should never say 'I'm sorry' for anything, because others will then perceive him to be weak."

I doubt if that is true with any leadership position, but I know it's not true with LifeGuards.

"True community cannot be experienced until group members take the risk of revealing their true selves to one another," says Jeffrey Arnold, Pennsylvania pastor, church planter, and author. And it is the leader who must model being transparent. Besides, rather than being repulsed, most crew members are drawn to the leader's transparency. Odds are they are struggling with the same kinds of difficulties.

Some of the marks of a transparent environment are confession, accep-

tance, repentance, and healing. Prayer takes on a completely different shape when people are being real.

Genesis 2:20-25 describes the open, honest relationship of a good marriage as becoming "one flesh." The terms used in this passage are also a picture of community. Adam and Eve were very open with one another ("they were naked and not ashamed") until sin entered the scene. Then they clothed themselves and hid behind bushes. Sin is what makes us ashamed and causes us to hide. Christ's death and resurrection, however, brings forgiveness. Remember, God is not evaluating us on

our performance. In LifeBoats, we too often play games and hide from each other.

Confession may be one key to removing the mask.

In a LifeBoat, if trust has been developed and there is an atmosphere of acceptance, intimacy happens naturally. But the worst thing you can do is to force intimacy upon people.

6 Ways to Encourage Intimacy

How do you deal with people who are afraid of intimacy? Perhaps you should start biblically by greeting one another with a holy kiss ... or maybe not. Seriously, folks need time to warm up to intimacy. But here are some things that might help.

1. The LifeGuard must model it, and it helps if your First Mate models it too.

2. Slightly deeper icebreakers that intensify gradually each week.

3. A proper response when a shipmate takes the plunge and opens up.

4. Pray that your crew will go to the next level of transparency.

5. Remind the LifeBoat about confidentiality and your covenant.

6. Keep it small. Once a crew grows to over six members, the intimacy level begins to plummet. If necessary, divide your crew for discussion.

Listening Skills

How to Open Your Ears & Really Hear

There are lots of courses and helps for learning listening, because listening is important. Just google "listening skills" for some quick tips.

The main idea is to remove distractions; make eye contact, but don't stare; and stop talking. Turn off your mobile phone! Distractions would include doodling, looking out the window, and picking your fingernails (picking your nose is really distracting, so please don't). Don't finish other people's sentences. Be patient, and let them finish their thought. Sometimes it's hard to verbalize feelings, abstract concepts, and spiritual things. It may take a few moments to find the right words. Ask for clarification on what you don't understand. Show empathy. Exhibit understanding. Listen also to their tone of voice and watch their body language.

Then respond. If they tell you about some pain in their life, it's okay to say, "That's terrible!" This isn't the old days when the therapist would sit with their notepad, scribbling impassively with a poker face no matter what was being shared. You're a LifeBoat, not a therapy session, so react! "Gosh, that's horrible!" "That's so wonderful, I want to dance a jig." "Man, that had to hurt."

Questioning Skills

Help People Discover Truth

Once the great Rabbi Solomon bar Isaac (AD 1040-1105) was asked why all the teaching rabbis would always answer a question with a question. He replied, "Why not?"

Jesus often used questions to teach, and questions to answer questions. He would also tell parables or illustrations, in which the point was not obvious, causing the hearer to ask their own questions.

Why not just give the answer? Wouldn't it be simpler and more direct? What effect would questions have on the learner? Would a discovered answer be more true than a direct answer? Why lean so heavily on questions?

Modern psychology has learned that it is much better for an individual to discover a truth than to be handed it. Often therapists will just keep asking questions until the patient finally discovers the answer that the therapist knew all along.

Asking the right questions causes a person to think through different options. In their minds they begin to look under different rocks, think through things they have never thought about before until they see something they haven't seen before. The teacher continues to ask questions, "Have you looked under this rock yet?" "Are there drawbacks to that option?" "Why would God want that?"

Questions that do not have an obvious answer, even questions with no "right" answers, work best at moving people to discovering truth.

A discovered truth is much more likely to be remembered than a truth that is taught directly. People are also more likely to apply a discovered truth. Since they discovered it, they take ownership of that truth, and it means more.

In today's Church, we are finding that the majority of people who learned much of their Bible knowledge in "just-feed-me" class situations are not involved in ministry today. They are not applying all that wonderful knowledge to their lives, nor are they using it to help others.

LifeBoats are an ideal situation for discovering truth. But leaders must restrain themselves from giving out the answers. Instead, it is better to keep asking questions until the mates come to the right conclusion.

Remember not to spoon-feed your crew. Instead, use questions to lead their minds to a ocean filled with truth.

Relationship-building Skills

Aka Friendship Skills

People who are popular and well-liked know how to approach other people, how to listen, to respond to needs, and to show appreciation for what the other has accomplished in a timely manner. Those who are well-liked have good communication skills and are capable of exchanging ideas, feelings, and concepts with others. They are genuinely cooperative and able to balance their own needs with the needs of others. They accept that the world is full of people who are different from them, and they see that as something that enriches their life. But these attributes are just the start for building friendships.

FRIENDSHIP SKILLS TO DEVELOP

1. Talk, Listen, Accept. Of course, honest and open communication is key. Listening is even more important. Acceptance of differences is a must.

2. Self-esteem, Self-control, Respect. Lack of self-control and self-esteem can ruin relationships, as can competitiveness, envy, and self-righteousness. In friendships, there is no excuse for slander or putting others down, however mildly. Any show of disrespect does untold damage. Don't be overly sensitive or quick to take offense either.

3. Choose to Be a Friend. No friendship is perfect; but if friends are committed to each other, their friendship can grow. Somewhere along the line you choose to befriend someone. It is a conscious choice. But it can never be a one-way street.

4. Energy and Risk. Making friends requires a lot of endeavor. Developing friendships is never easy nor straightforward. Initially it involves taking risks that one's ideas or actions will be rejected.

5. Time and Effort. Making friends requires time and energy. In our busy world, the main reason people don't have friends is a lack of willingness to invest in friendships. Keeping in touch is work.

6. Laugh Together. Enjoying each other's presence strengthens a friendship. Laugh long, laugh hard. When tension develops between friends, nothing helps like a little comic relief to put things in perspective.

7. Adventure Together. Experiencing new things with others builds friendships. Take a hike, a sail, a trip to a new restaurant. Work a project together. If you do something together that limits communication, like seeing a movie, be sure to take some time afterwards to debrief. Hear each other's reactions to what you just experienced.

8. Give and Take. Friendship is the willingness and ability to participate in give-and-take, back-and-forth, reciprocal communication. Any of us who have ever had an "All-About-ME" friend know just how important this skill is to keep the relationship healthy.

9. Be a Trusted Friend. Don't talk bad, or gossip, about your friend. Don't make jokes at their expense. Don't be mean or stab others in the back. Defend. Keep secrets. Tell the truth. Keep promises and agreements. Keep commitments. And be loyal.

10. Be There. This involves offering comfort in times of need. Accept invitations.

11. Don't Demand Perfection. Allow your friends to be human and even to make mistakes.

12. Be Open. Practice self-disclosure. Share.

13. Apologize. Make amends and negotiate conflicts.

14. Be Considerate and Polite. Don't dominate. Talk about things that interest your friend, not just things that interest you. Don't talk over them, interrupt, or seek to be the center of attention. Be interested, ask open questions, and try to find out more. Be respectful and sensitive to their feelings. Think before you speak (try not to upset or offend). Don't pick needless arguments. Try to understand the perspective of others. Don't just assume that you are right and they are wrong. Don't put them down. Don't judge and stereotype people. Don't try to control them. Give choices.

15. Be Like a Detective. Discover what your friend likes, values, what makes them who they are. Notice what they are good at and not too good at. Find out about the baggage from their past — we all have baggage. Ask your friend to talk. Ask them what they are thinking, feeling. Be receptive.

Encouraging Skills

The Barnabas Factor

In several of his letters to the New Testament churches, the Apostle Paul writes, "I thank God for you because..." (Colossians 1:3; 1 Thessalonians 1:2, 2:13, 3:9; 2 Thessalonians 1:3, 2:13; and 2 Timothy 1:3). Encouragement often comes in the form of thanksgiving expressed through a prayer or a note. Take a friend aside, look them in the eye, and say, "Thank you so much for being..."

You encourage people by recognizing what they are doing right. The letters to the churches in Revelation point mostly to the things the churches need to work on, but this criticism is not before the encouragement. "I know your deeds, your hard work and your perseverance" (Revelation 2:2).

I saw a first-grade teacher once point out a girl who was doing it right: "Look at how Jill is quietly sitting upright in her chair with her books in order." Immediately the other kids in the room ran to their chairs, straightened their books, got quiet and sat upright. Wow, that worked a lot better than yelling at the kids to sit down and shut up.

To the church at Smyrna, the Revelator writes, "I know your afflictions and your poverty—yet you are rich! I know about the slander you are enduring" (Revelation 2:9). Simply letting people know that you are keenly aware of what they are going through is encouraging. Somehow it motivates people to keep moving through the hardship.

People are different, so different forms of encouragement have differing degrees of effectiveness depending on personal preferences. A good discussion topic at a LifeBoat meeting would begin with the question, "When have you been encouraged by someone?" Your crew's answers will give you insight on how best to encourage them. The discussion would probably also inspire them to be more encouraging to others.

We could learn something from the way a football team freely high-fives, slaps shoulder pads and helmets, and yells approval during a game. It's encouraging their teammates. I have this secret belief that anytime a teenager leads worship (reads the Scripture, sings a solo, or when the youth choir performs), they should get a standing ovation from the congregation.

One trick is to remember the Golden Rule. Figure out what encourages you, and then do those same things for others. Also act quickly. If an encouraging thought comes to mind, move on it immediately. If you wait, it may not have the same effect later. "Encourage one another daily, as long as it is called today..." (Hebrews 3:13).

I like to add a few words of praise when I'm introducing someone. I point out why it's a privilege to know this person, and how knowing them has benefited me. Not only does it encourage them to be complimented in front of others, but it sets up the new relationship to succeed.

When someone is hurting, write a note telling them that you are praying for them. You might want to include the prayer as well. Just write it out. Remind them of God's promises. Remind them that He is a loving God full of mercy and grace.

Don't forget to celebrate. Small celebrations for small things (a note, coffee together, a phone call). Big celebrations for big victories (a special meal, a party, a gift).

And don't forget to tell people how they have encouraged you.

Thrill Skills

Don't Get Bored

In her fiftieth wedding anniversary speech, a wife reminisced, "When I married him, he told me that he couldn't promise me riches or an easy life. But he did promise that we would never be bored. And it has been anything but boring. He kept that promise."

To have a long-term successful Life-Boat, you must keep it exciting. This will take imagination and a willingness to try new things. Fight the rut. By default, a crew will start doing things the same way every week. The only thing that should be a constant is change.

Here are three things you don't want to forget. I could make a long list of suggested activities with each, but that in itself would be boring. So I'll just give one example, the best example, for each.

1. Don't Forget the Fun Factor.

The LifeGuard couldn't believe that the crew didn't know what it meant to paper someone. So he explained that it's when you go to their house and throw toilet paper over all their trees, cars, and house. It must be done late at night and quietly so the folks don't see it till the next morning. The dew needs a chance to do its thing. It

makes a mess to clean up but doesn't really hurt anything. Besides it can be quite pretty if done right.

The LifeBoat set aside a Friday night a few weeks away to paper the pastor's house (it's one of those things pastors can expect when called to the pastorate — a sort of persecution, a testing of patience). But then the LifeGuard secretly organized the deacons of the church to be ready.

On the night of the dastardly deed, the LifeBoat parked their cars several streets away, loaded up with all the toilet paper they could carry, and headed in stealth mode to the pastor's home. They lined up across the front yard preparing to throw.

They got through one roll, when the garage door opened and out charged the deacons launching water balloons. Toilet paper is no match for water. Luckily it was a warm night.

Needless to say, it took a while to rebuild the trust factor between the Life-Guard and his LifeBoat. But oh, how they laughed.

2. Don't Forget the Surprise Factor.

Boy, were they surprised when halfway through the LifeBoat meeting, the mayor arrived. Their First Mate had some contacts and had arranged for her to come by. She told them about some of her close friendships and seemed impressed at their commitment to one another. It was a good and memorable encounter.

3. Don't Forget the Challenge Factor.

The challenge put to the women's LifeBoat was to conduct bingo night at the state mental health hospital — the institution where they kept the severely mentally ill. For this crew of Christian country gals, this was going to be different and totally out of their comfort zone. But they accepted the challenge.

On the first bingo night, one of the male patients said in a sarcastic voice, "Oh boy, bingo. How exciting."

At which one of the nice church ladies asked, "Well, what would you like to do instead?"

He responded very matter of fact. "Sex. That's what I'd like to do. Sex is exciting. Bingo is not."

The shipmates of that LifeBoat learned to respond with humor and grace in these situations. They came away with lots of stories like that one and their bingo nights were far from boring.

How to Sink a LifeBoat

I know this whole idea scares the tar out of some of you. The very thought of opening up and being real, of actually sharing your thoughts and feelings is new and frightening. For many of you reading this book, the concept is too exotic. The idea of taking on someone else's problems sounds ludicrous. Then allowing people to push you is counter-intuitive, even if it's pushing you toward what God wants in your life. But to me, this is the difference between playing church and really being a church. It's the difference between what many churches call fellowship (church dinners, ice cream socials, and softball) and the true fellowship the New Testament says we believers

will share.

But I need to be more understanding. For you all who just don't get it, I need to give you a way out. So this chapter is for those of you who can't tolerate the idea of LifeBoats. Just in case you accidentally find yourself in a LifeBoat and you can't jump ship, here are some ways you can sink it.

Break Confidentiality

Hands down, this is the best and fastest way to sink a LifeBoat. As they said during the World Wars, "Loose lips sink ships."

People are starting to open up, con-

LIFEBOAT SURVIVAL STORY
"LifeBoat Junkie"

Jon was always kind of gawky. Trying to have a conversation with him was awkward, as he was very limited in his social abilities and relational skills. He was introverted, too, and seemed uncomfortable around people, which in turn made people uncomfortable around him.

The truth was that no one really knew much about Jon, beyond that he was a professional and married with children.

When our church launched LifeBoats, I don't think any of us expected Jon to jump in — at least not without a floatation device. And yet, he tried it out. The members of that first LifeBoat did an exceptional job of including him, making sure he didn't stand alone during refreshment time, and giving him space to express himself and open up.

Over the years, we watched him emerge from behind his wall of social unease. The experience of being in a boat actually made him an addict. At one time, he was attending three LifeBoats!

I think Jon recognized a flaw in himself, and he saw LifeBoats as an opportunity to help push past that weakness. What ultimately happened was a beautiful thing. Jon began to talk about his personal struggles, and he began to grow spiritually. He was a source of strength and support to the other mates in his LifeBoats, and God became important to him.

The result was addictive, and Jon was the first LifeBoat junkie I've come across.

WARNING: LIFEBOATS CAN BE HABIT FORMING!

fess their fears, share their most painful moments, and talk about their struggles. Then some guy blabs, and that ends that. Folks just quit coming, or if they do come, nobody is sharing.

The old joke illustrates it beautifully:

For years the three pastors in town went fishing together every Thursday. One day, one pastor said, "You know, we've been doing this for a long time and I think we've come to trust each other. I think we should confess our sins to one another."

One pastor answered, "Okay, I'll start. I'll confess to you that I've been involved in an adulterous affair. Wow! That felt good to finally tell someone."

It was the second pastor's turn, so he said, "I'm a drunk. No one knows it, but I drink myself to sleep every night. Can't help myself."

At this, the third pastor picks up the oars and vigorously starts rowing the boat back to shore.

"Hey, what are you doing? It's your turn to confess!"

He just kept rowing and said, "I'm a gossip, and I can't wait to get back to town!"

Breaking confidentially doesn't just sink a LifeBoat, it blows it out of the water. I believe this is why the New Testament is so against gossip. The early Church was comprised of small groups — LifeBoats — and gossip devastates LifeBoats.

Breaking confidentiality kills the very trust that takes so long to build within a community. And trust is very hard to win back. That's why Jesus made adultery the only out in a marriage. It kills the trust factor in the marriage, and it's nearly impossible to get it back.

To avoid this, many LifeBoats discuss confidentiality at length. Some lay down the law: "Anything discussed here is top secret. You can't tell anyone, ever!" Others find it beneficial to talk it out some, to clarify any confusion. "What if I'm court-ordered to divulge? Must I serve jail time rather than tell?"

As we said before, common sense is the rule. But a suitable conversation about what is confidential and what isn't will be helpful. And that discussion needs to happen sooner rather than later.

Once I was asked, "Hey, what did Bob tell you guys at your LifeBoat meeting last night? You can trust me. I'm just worried about him."

So I asked, "Can you keep a secret?"

"Yes, of course."

"So can I," I replied.

Dealing with Broken Confidence

How to do you deal with a broken confidence after the damage is done? There are no easy answers on this one. It will depend on what was shared, where it was shared, how many people are involved, and so on. But start by confronting the gossip (that's what we'll call the offender, because that's what the New Testament calls that offense).

Let's say at a church prayer meeting you hear a crew mate in your LifeBoat break a confidence as a prayer request (believe me, it happens). Quietly take that shipmate aside immediately (yes, in the middle of the meeting, even in the middle of the prayer). "Excuse me, but I need to speak to you in the hall." Once out of the ear shot of others, quickly point out the error. Focus on the behavior, not the motive (the intention may well have been good, who knows). "I think our friend wanted *us* to pray about that, *not* the whole church. She told us that at LifeBoat, and remember LifeBoat is supposed to be confidential. How can we fix this?"

Now, let's switch roles. Let's say you're the one who just got busted. How do you respond? Start damage control immediately. Assess the best way to do that, but don't waste time over-thinking it. You might want to go right back into that meeting and confess and ask for help. "Listen, I just told you something that I had no business telling you. Joann told me that in confidence, and I just broke that confidence. Will you please help me here and not take it out of this room? Please!"

The next thing you'll need to do is let Joann know as soon as possible what has happened. Confess your sin to the person you offended, and try and work it out with them. Don't allow them to let you off the hook too easy. They may say, "No worries! Shake it off." But you need to push and ask again and again, "How can I fix this?" Focus on the behavior, not the motive, because we don't really know our own heart.

"I don't know what I was thinking, but I really blew it."

So let's review the steps:

- ❖ Confront the gossip

- ❖ Focus on behavior, not motive

- ❖ Start damage control immediately

- ❖ Confess and ask for help

- ❖ Confess to the individual offended

- ❖ Make amends

- ❖ Pray it through

That example was less complicated than most because it was caught early, the motive seemed innocent, and the damage was easier to control. But the principles are the same for more serious breaches. From Jesus' teachings, we draw some guidelines: (1) Deal with behaviors (actions and the fruits of the actions), not the motives, because we can't judge even our own hearts, much less someone else's. (2) Keep the circle (of people involved) as small as possible, as long as possible (Matthew 18). It may be that everyone in your LifeBoat need not be involved. You surely wouldn't kick someone out of your LifeBoat for the above offense. But if the behavior didn't stop, or the gossip is killing the trust factor in your group, you might need to take harsh steps to restore the trust. Asking the gossip to leave the crew may be the only unfortunate solution. The question is, to what extent is the gossip affecting the trust level in the LifeBoat?

I knew one LifeBoat that couldn't face making a crew mate walk the plank. And yet their LifeBoat was crippled by trust be-trayal, so they disbanded the whole crew. A few months later, they formed a new LifeBoat with all the original shipmates … except for the gossip. I still don't know whether to call that clever or cowardly.

Maintain Superficiality

Superficiality — all LifeBoats start out in this mode, just skimming the surface. Exchanging names. Being polite. Niceties are observed. Lots of discussions around the weather, sports, and the stock market. We're discovering common interests, finding out facts about family, employment, and locations lived. Playing it safe. Feeling out the trust levels, checking the temperature of the water. Every now and then, a crew member will dip below the surface, test-flying minor projectiles, to assess the response. This experimenting is a nonchalant, subtle way of asking, "Can I trust you?"

Bill Hybels calls it pseudo-community. It's the illusion of community. It's basically the exchange of information. No one is venturing deeper into matters of the heart. No one is rocking the boat. No one is sharing their pain.

It's what the Internet and social networking is good for. In fact, the age groups that really love Facebook and HootSuite are up to their necks in this info-only pseudo-community. It serves to give them a thirst for real relationships. When this group joins a face-to-face LifeBoat, it better dive deep fast or it will lose them, because they have plenty of the other surface stuff in their lives. They're looking for something that will satisfy their desire for true community.

There's nothing *super* about being superficial. No admission of fear or hurt feelings. It's safe. No straying too far from the sidewalk.

"Boy, the Dow is really responding to the jobless rate!"

"Hey, you think our LifeBoat could beat the Redskins this year?"

"Gee, that really sounds painful, but we've got to get going with our Bible study. We want to finish Ephesians by the end of the month."

Maintaining superficiality will eventually sink a LifeBoat, but not as fast as breaking confidentiality. That's a shipwreck, whereas superficiality is a slow running aground. The LifeBoat slowly drifts to shore, beaches on the coast, and dries up.

To stay afloat in deep waters, a Life-Boat must move from pseudo-commu-nity to true community. It can't remain a benign little party that gathers over tea and biscuits and then scatters. It can't stay a safe group that hides behind Bible study.

Oh, don't get me wrong. I love the Bible, and I love studying and reaping all I can from it for guidance in my life. But too many LifeBoats let the Bible study overtake their time together. LifeBoats are for taking the masks off, for sharing our fears, feelings, frustrations, and failures. It's challenging each other to get past casual Christianity.

All LifeBoats begin superficially, but if they stay that way it will destroy them. If you're just going through the motions, you're merely paddle-boating around the resort lake. It's relaxing and the scenery is lovely, but eventually, you and your crew mates will get bored.

Warning! Warning! If your plan is to run your LifeBoat aground by maintaining superficiality, I need to warn you. It only takes one member of your crew to risk

We were all hurting; we all shared his shame. Over the next couple of months, I saw this LifeBoat pour out love to this man and his wife and his daughter like I'd never seen before.

Once you experience that depth, you can never go back to the puddles. Once you've tasted what it's like to be in a real, deep community, you never want to face life without it again.

disclosure, and your plan will dissolve.

I was in a LifeBoat once that was hopelessly stuck in its superficiality. I was about to give up on it. The deep ocean wasn't anywhere in sight. We'd been boating for a year, and I figured it might be another year before we got past shallow waters, if then.

But then Rich came in one evening with his head down. He didn't even let the meeting get started properly before he blurted out, "I got to tell ya'll something." (Rich was from Tennessee.) "My daughter got arrested this morning." The crew pulled their chairs in closer as he recounted the story. But he gave us more than just the facts. He told how scared he was. Then he talked at length about the shame he felt. I had never heard anyone talk firsthand about shame before. In two hours that LifeBoat surged from pseudo to real. I remember how amazed he was that none of his shipmates indicated judgment in the slightest. The women in the group wept. The men sighed and groaned in sympathy.

There've been times in my LifeBoat when I've walked in and said, "Guys, I need to vent. I need a half hour." They'd sit back with that there-he-goes-again look on their faces, and I'd unload my frustration. I'd dump the whole truckload. I'd rant about family, or church, or work. I'd express my disappointment or my confusion. And when I'd finally wound down, they'd pray. Then pray some more. Then finally, I'd be in a state in which I could pray.

This kind of sharing bonds us together. It's freeing.

I wouldn't trade anything for my LifeBoat. The one place where I can be honest, where I can say without fear, "I'm blowing it in several areas, but maybe with your help I can lick it."

Unsteady Sailing

Another way to sink a LifeBoat is to be inconsistent and overdue in meeting. This is probably the easiest way to get rid of a LifeBoat. Don't make it a priority, and if anything else comes up, blow off the LifeBoat. "We'll see you next week ... if nothing better comes up." You can always find something else that is going on. After all, we live in an overactive world.

"Oh, sorry. There's poetry reading on Mondays, handball on Tuesdays, and some really good shows on TV on Wednesday nights..."

"Weekends are impossible."

"Sunday night? No, after hitting church on Sunday morning, we're toast the rest of the day."

"Thursday night, sure. But remember, that's the night I work late, so we can't be there till 8 or 8:15. And oh, yeah, I get up early on Fridays to run, so I hope the meeting doesn't go past nine."

"Anything mid-November to mid-January is a wash. The holidays, you know."

"The winter months are iffy. We better not plan anything, because the weather could cancel it unexpectedly."

"March Madness kills meeting that month, and April is tax time, so we'd better wait."

"Our summers are for vacations and team sports."

"September and October are my busy season at work, so I need to drop out those months."

"Can't meet next week. It's my son's basketball tournament."

"Aren't the Olympics starting?"

Actually, you don't have to find an excuse to never meet. Just space it out so there are several weeks between meetings.

What happens is everyone has to review and restate their situation again, because memories turn fuzzy over time. Also, people have to get reacquainted all over again. "Did you say you have one kid or two?" "Oh, that was you? I got you confused with a coworker."

But the main thing that prolonging the time in between meetings accomplishes is that it damages the healthy life cycle of a LifeBoat. It lengthens the amount of time it takes for the friendships to take form — the moment when the LifeBoat bonds and it becomes an organism, a unified community. It also stretches the time it takes for the trust levels to increase.

Don't Resolve Conflicts

It's a given: There will be skirmishes in a LifeBoat. It's inevitable.

The man who taught me to sail when I was a teenager, gave me some free (and somewhat sexist) dating advice. In his rough, salty voice, he warned me, "You look at these pretty little things so sweet and nice. Well, put them on a boat for a day. Let the sun beat down on them during the hottest part of the afternoon. Let the salt water spray hit their face and tangle their hair. Let them get hot and miserable. Watch their makeup start to run. And that sweet little thing will start to get mean. She'll get downright nasty."

Well, so much for dating advice. But I can tell you that if you LifeBoat with people long enough, the boat can get to feeling pretty small. When you start to do life together, the sun will get hot, and you'll see your shipmates on their bad days as well as their good days. When you start getting honest with each other, their makeup will run and their masks will fall off.

Two crew mates will develop a bit of friction between them. Someone is too talkative or always late or overly dramatic. Someone will break a promise once too often. And the tension will build. If you

stuff it, ignore it, or smooth it over with a bandage, it will undermine the whole lifeboat.

Very seldom did Jesus give us a formula, a one-two-three-step plan. But He does just that in Matthew 18 for solving conflicts among believers. Now I've seen people use this formula to beat the heck out of people, but the actual purpose of the plan is to bring reconciliation. And if that isn't your motive for following the steps, then Matthew 18 turns into a weapon. A pretty solid weapon at that. "Sorry this is killing you, but I'm just following the Bible," says the Pharisee.

As a side note, I think Jesus wouldn't be disappointed at all if you repeat the first step (go to the person one-on-one) a few times until you're sure it isn't going to work. I'll even push it more and suggest you try the second step (go to that person

with a second peacemaker) more than once as well. Let me push a tad more, get real spiritual here, and tell you you'd better soak this whole process in prayer. 'Cause you can't resolve conflict successfully on your own. The Holy Spirit has to intervene. The Spirit is the One who will do the reconciling here.

And while I'm pushing, let me add one more suggestion. Paul said to correct each other in love. That doesn't mean saying, "I love you, but..." It means that you have proved your love over and over before you attempt to correct. Then a person is more likely to hear your correction.

The reason for LifeBoats is spiritual growth, and learning conflict management is part of that process. Sort through skirmishes, and don't shrink from this.

I remember Craig taking Mike aside. "I don't like the way you keep embarrassing your wife. It's driving me crazy. It's embarrassing me. You probably don't even realize what you're doing."

Notice he didn't correct him in front of the group, nor in front of his wife, but in private. He was saying, "This is between you and me." Notice also that he didn't attack the man's motives; he even gives him an excuse ("you probably don't even realize"). Instead he focused on the behavior, the result ("embarrassing your wife"), and his feelings ("it's embarrassing me and driving me crazy"). Craig's learned a lot over the years about handling conflict. The question now is, what has Mike learned about taking correction?

I can recall several times when someone was rubbing me the wrong way. Unfortunately it took me years to discover that I handled conflict poorly by avoiding it. I look back now and I'm horrified at the littered path of broken relationships — relationships that might have been saved if I had acted instead of letting it slide.

When I consider this, two situations come to mind when I did speak up. Once, it didn't work; it takes two to do the dance. But the other time it did work. We were able to rescue the relationship and the LifeBoat.

More often than not, these situations pushed me to my knees and I ended up crying out, "I'm the problem!"

Run at the First Sign of Invasion

Another way to sink a LifeBoat is to run when the crew turns on you. This is not possible when the LifeBoat is first launching or even a couple months into the journey. But it is a very effective method of destruction a year or two in, when the relationships are solid. It will happen when the level of trust is elevated and the LifeBoat is moving into deeper spiritual waters.

There will come a time when the others in your LifeBoat will identify a compromise in your spiritual life. It will be in your blind spot — something you've subconsciously closed your eyes to. But your crew mates will see it. Probably the others in your life see it too, but they write it off, thinking, "Well, that's just Joe. It's just the way he is. He can't help it." We close our eyes to it, but our LifeBoat won't. They won't wink at it like everyone else. They won't gloss over it. While everybody else just slaps you on the back and says, "Boys will be boys," your shipmates will be plotting how best to point it out to you.

They've waited until the time is right. They've waited until the relationships are sturdy — when you know that they love you and that they'll love you whether you change or not. They've proved that again and again.

Now they ask you about it. They put their noses in your business. They start climbing walls that you've clearly marked, "No Trespassing. High Voltage. Danger. Stay Away!"

Life in the LifeBoat gets uncomfortable quickly. You think, *Why are they doing this to me? I hate these LifeBoats. I don't need these guys in my face.*

They continue to push. "How can you say you love your wife when you're rarely home romancing her?"

The discomfort is overwhelming. You fight. You rationalize. But they know you, and they see through your lies.

Now you see it. This is your chance to sink this LifeBoat. All you've got to do is run. Jump ship. Leave them in your wake. Paul Simon starts singing, "There must be fifty ways to leave your LifeBoat."

The prophet Nathan and King David had a close relationship. One day Nathan comes to David and tells him a little story about a man who had hundreds of sheep of his own, and yet he stole another man's one and only sheep, because he wanted one more. David demands to know who this thief is so he can execute justice. At which Nathan points to David. "Thou art the man!" (2 Samuel 12).

David was the king; he could have killed Nathan on the spot. Nathan risked everything revealing David's sin to him. But Nathan loved God so much and he loved David so much that he pointed out what David wanted to keep hidden.

When Nathan did this, he served David well. And your Life-Boat is serving you well. Don't jump ship. Yes, it hurts, but don't get defensive and run away. Respond.

It will knock you down, but they will help you up. And you'll be stronger for it in the end.

Stay Self-serving

Here's another way to gradually sink your LifeBoat: Keep the focus inward. It makes good sense to spend most of your time focusing on the lives of your fellow crew, especially when a LifeBoat is first launched. But keeping that focus will eventually sink your boat. It comes to a stage where you can predict how everyone in your crew will respond every time, no matter what comes to light. You've gotten to know them, which is good, but you've also heard them play all their tapes multiple times, which is downright boring. You've heard all their stories, all their opinions, and now every meeting is repeat, repeat, repeat.

You try to change the subject, but what subject have you not already covered several times over? You know what's important to them — their political stance, their families, their backgrounds, what makes them tick.

What keeps it fresh? Exciting? The key is to turn the focus outward. Yes, make sure that you know each other, that you're caring for each other, and that you're pushing each other. But also turn around and face out. Find a cause or Kingdom work to invest in.

Also, invite new people. All LifeBoats need new winds from time to time.

Try to determine what's the best size crew for your LifeBoat. That will depend on the personalities of the crew. Some folks are good with a crew of three or four, and some better with eight to ten. Then move the LifeBoat to comprise that number. You probably can handle one or two more people in your boat. When a shipmate moves away or drifts away, think about who next to invite.

There will be times when you need to close your LifeBoat for a while. If a crew mate is going through a really rough time, it might not be appropriate to assimilate a new crew member. But don't keep it closed for too long.

The default position for most Life-Boats is turned inward, so you need to be intentional about focusing outward. Your LifeBoat will probably need to discuss this

---

Captain's Orders

"Fish till the boat is full, then get another boat."

balance on occasion.

But Please Don't Sink the LifeBoat

We've covered several ways to sink a LifeBoat ... but please don't. Ships carry lifeboats for one reason — in case the ship sinks. So we don't need lifeboats that sink, and we don't even want them to leak.

D. L. Moody used to say, "This world is a sinking ship, and our job is not to keep it from sinking, but to get as many people off the ship as possible." He, of course, was talking about salvation. But I think we can expand the metaphor to say, "If you live on this ship called earth, you need to get in a LifeBoat."

In my college days, I had a friend we called Thunder. Whenever you showed him the "A" you got on a term paper, or your new car, or your new television, or even the new sanctuary at your church, he'd take the wind right out of your sails by saying, "It's all gonna burn, man, it's all gonna burn."

He was referring to 2 Peter 3:10-13, which tells us how it's all going down, how "the elements will melt with a fervent heat" (by the way, that's a good description of a thermal nuclear explosion).

The followup question is, what are you doing in your life that isn't going up in smoke? Well, things are not going to last, but people will. So invest in people. And the best way to do that is to develop friendships.

Thus the LifeBoat.

LIFEBOAT SURVIVAL STORY
"Raised by the Committee"

We lived half the country away from my grandparents when I was a kid, so I didn't grow up with the benefit of extended family around. But my parents had a LifeBoat — six couples all from the same church. They called themselves "The Committee."

I was raised by the Committee. They were like extra parents; their kids were like my stand-in cousins. (Not quite like siblings, since I already had two of those, and two was plenty.) It seemed like I spent as much time at their homes as my own. It was these extra parents that gave me jobs when I was a teenager, prayed me through college, and referenced me for jobs when I was grown.

I grew up watching this LifeBoat love and support one another. In fact, I think the reason I am so convinced that God is love is because these six couples modeled it to me. One of "my cousins" died tragically in his twenties, and I watched the Committee surround his parents with more care than I'd ever seen before. One of my secondary moms passed away, then her spouse (one of my secondary dads) died eighteen months later. Even though their kids were in their upper teens and twenties, I saw my parents unofficially adopt them, and the Committee filled in however possible for their loss.

I watched this LifeBoat laugh together, enjoy life together, hurt together, support one another ... together. My extra parents taught me things about life that I would have never listened to or accepted from my parents.

Take it from me, who was raised by the Committee. LifeBoating is good for your kids, too. It's not taking quality time from them ... it's multiplying it.

Troubleshooting

Troubleshooting Tip No. 1
THE TALKER

I loved him and knew he wanted to share, but we were short on time. Stan, the Talker, had come alive. I felt helpless.

Have you ever experienced that? The Talker is one who dominates the meeting. They are common. Even Jesus had to contend with His Talker — the outspoken, impulsive Peter. There are ways to handle the Talker and help him outgrow his unhealthy desire to constantly talk.

Remember, there is always a root behind excessive talking. Most of the time it is the need for attention. Give them loving attention and show you care, but at the same time, be firm about simple guidelines for sharing in the LifeBoat.

Here are a couple of things to try: (1) Be strategic about where you sit. Eye contact gives permission to speak, so sit *beside* the Talker. (You can also draw out the quiet person by sitting across from them.) (2) Just say it out loud. "Some of us have been doing all the talking. Let's hear the insights of those who have been listening." (3) Meet privately with the Talker and share with them that their talkativeness reduces the opportunity for ministry and the feeling of ownership for others. Most Talk-

ers have never been confronted about their problem. Remember the root cause of this disorder, and pray about the confrontation first. You'll need the Holy Spirit for this to work and to be loving at the same time. (4) If the problem persists, meet with the Talker again and devise a hand signal to let them know that they are over-talking.

Sometimes the Talker is the LifeGuard. LifeBoat leaders need to continually monitor themselves to make sure they don't start monopolizing the group discussion. A reality check with a trusted member of your LifeBoat helps. Just ask them every now and then: "Am I talking too much? Am I moving out of the way enough for the crew to discuss?"

If you feel you have a tendency to dominate conversations, ask a crew member for help. Agree on a sign they can give if you start moving in that direction. Whenever I'm facilitating a group dialogue, I like to keep asking myself, *Why am I talking?* Once I remember silently praying, "Lord, help me to keep my mouth shut."

Troubleshooting Tip No. 2
THE ANSWER MAN

It was almost comical. We had been invited to a pastor's home to meet the new youth minister at his church. As we drove over, I mentioned to my wife that this would be a good evening for us to sit and soak, because the other three couples invited were some of the smartest people in the city — maybe even the state. One was considered an expert in church growth, and he had the track record to prove it. Another I had great respect for, because she had established an excellent student ministry at a state college and now was directing some forty college ministers across our state.

Well, obviously no one had warned this young man, who was new to the area, because he launched into how no one was doing church or student ministry right and he knew exactly what really needed to happen. He talked and talked. He actually talked down to us. No one got a word in edgewise. Not that we wanted to speak up, because he clearly had all the answers. He wasn't looking for confirmation or other opinions. He was there to teach us, not to learn. His ideas were not bad; it was his unteachable spirit that rubbed us the wrong way. I wasn't too surprised later when I learned he'd lost his job after only a few months.

Nothing stifles conversation like the guy who sees everything as black or white and is so sure he knows the correct answer to most everything. It's really obnoxious when they abruptly end every discussion with a trite little platitude and say it like that settles it and nobody should be fool enough to question their answer. The Know-It-All can really stifle a discussion.

Frankly, this can be hard to deal with. The cause of this flaw is usually a feeling of inferiority that must be covered with a fake confidence. Sometimes it's a product of an unsure faith. The inner fear is that any doubt would cause their whole faith structure to collapse, so they must overstate things to eliminate any weak spots.

What might work to stop the Answer Man is "yes, and" and "yes, if" statements. But more often than not, the person leading the discussion needs to signal that it's time to hear other options, other opinions, or other points of view.

As with the Talker, sometimes the Answer Man is the LifeGuard. They can begin to see themselves as the expert, and so they listen patiently to everyone's opinion then end the talk by stating the official answer — theirs. Other times, the LifeGuard will study and study the topic before the meeting and simply must tell you everything they learned. If your LifeGuard is tending to do this, start by taking them aside and pointing it out. "You probably don't even know you're doing this, but..."

Troubleshooting Tip No. 3
EXTRA GRACE REQUIRED

In the chapter titled "Picking Your Crew," we addressed "The Stability Factor." But sometimes folks who need more help than a LifeBoat can provide (who need professional help) end up in a LifeBoat. This unfortunately doesn't serve anyone.

Some churches have formed EGR LifeBoats; these are for those folks who require extra grace. This frees up the other LifeBoats for smoother sailing. The LifeGuards of EGR LifeBoats need to be skilled, patient, and loving. Of course, you don't call it an EGR LifeBoat officially. That's code talk for the insiders to know.

The way to start an EGR LifeBoat is to first find an able LifeGuard that can handle this kind of crew and has the gifting for its unique challenges. Some pastoral counselors are great at leading EGR groups.

This would be an invitation-only LifeBoat. The target crew mate would be those who have a real desire to be in a LifeBoat — perhaps they've joined or tried to join a healthy crew — but who need that special grace. The Bosun has probably heard from other LifeGuards who might be in need of a EGR LifeBoat.

If the individual is already in a LifeBoat, the new LifeGuard may approach the EGR shipmate, saying, "I'm starting a new LifeBoat, and I'd like you to be a seed member to help me launch it."

It's best if these LifeBoats stay small, three or four people at most, because what happens is the LifeGuard needs to give lots of individual attention to each crew mate. It really is like several two-person LifeBoats (the LifeGuard and each crew member) that come together regularly, maybe monthly, for a corporate gathering.

Troubleshooting Tip No. 4
DEFUSING AN ANGRY CREW MEMBER

Chances are you will rarely encounter a person who is extremely angry at your church. However, when a crew member does become angry, you, as the LifeGuard, need to know how to defuse the situation. Failure to act decisively risks losing the individual to the LifeBoat, the church, maybe even to God.

First, understand the situation.

The first and most important step is to put the "blowup" into perspective and to see it from the other person's point of view. There are several points to remember:

1. According to Lyle Sussman, author and Ph.D., there is only one reason a rational person becomes irate. They are "trying to tell you, 'I matter.' When a person's sense of self-worth is diminished, it makes that person feel unimportant." Seeing that the message of the church is "You matter to God and therefore you matter to us," we need to attempt to communicate that any way we can. The first way to communicate caring is to listen, and listen carefully.

2. All complaints are rational from the perspective of the person lodging them. Try to look at your LifeBoat or your church from the perspective of the angry person, rather than from your perspective.

3. The person's willingness to raise the issue says that they want to keep the relationship with you, the LifeBoat, and the church. The person who will take the time to complain wants to correct the situation.

4. Complaints are not personal attacks. So don't take the anger personally. Even if you are directly at fault, they get angry because they are frustrated and because they want problems solved.

Second, focus on solutions.

Once you have the situation in proper perspective, take appropriate action to address the problem. Jesus gives us some hints on how to handle situations like this in Matthew 18:15ff. There are three steps: *contain, qualify,* and *correct.*

1. Contain the problem. Jesus' principle here seems to be to keep the number of people involved as small as possible for as long as possible. First go privately. If that doesn't work, take one or two others with you. If it still doesn't work, expand the involvement to the church.

Once the angry person involves you, *you are involved,* so start by listening carefully. You can't solve a problem if you don't know what the problem is in the first place. Do not interrupt. When a person is angry, they need to complete their thoughts, and it's usually hard to articulate anything when you're angry. They generally vent first, then they begin to define the problem.

2. Qualify the problem. Jesus tells us to go and talk it out. During this phase, ask additional questions. This not only helps to get to the root cause of the problem (they may be transferring), but further defuses the person's anger.

3. Correct the problem (action phase). Once you have identified the problem and its cause(s), you can take steps to solve it.

Troubleshooting Tip No. 5
MEMBERS WITH THEIR OWN AGENDA

It's true that groups can turn poisonous. A person that "has it in for the pastor" or is totally against the direction the church is moving in can use the LifeBoat ministry to win recruits. It's a great field to plant nega-

tive seeds. So how do you identify this and how do you respond to it?

You want people to feel free to speak their opinions, but when you see a pattern of negativity developing, you know you have a problem. If the subject keeps coming up or you find yourself defending the church a lot, there may be a toxin operating in your LifeBoat.

Of course, prevention is always better than damage control. So building a positive culture in your LifeBoat early on is important. To build favorable habits among your crew, you must educate and model. Teach people early on that the purpose of your LifeBoat is to care for each other and to spur one another to grow in Christ. State very directly that this LifeBoat is not about running the church, setting its direction, or keeping all the staff in line. There are committees, teams, and church leadership that are tasked with that. "If anything, we are about supporting and building up the church." Make this a keynote early on and repeat it regularly.

It's also important to teach your LifeBoat the potential dangers of including people with their own agendas. Ask your crew, "When does a LifeBoat turn to poison?" These kinds of discussions will help and motivate LifeBoats to monitor themselves. It will help them see where a conversation is going while they can change its direction.

As we stated in chapter one,

People often get sucked into messages before they realize what is happening because they have never been taught otherwise. In fact, a healthy church is one in which the congregation speaks up and says, "Hey, we don't talk like that around here. That is not what our church is about. If we have a problem with something, we go talk it out directly with the leader that can do something about it. We don't assault others with our negative dialogue."

Over the years, I have learned the hard way that simply saying, "You need to talk to the pastor about that," doesn't work. Usually the disgruntled person will not go and talk to someone who can actually do something about their complaint. It's like spreading the negative energy is more satisfying to them than solving the problem or talking it out with someone in authority.

I have learned since then to say, "Look, that is not something we discuss in this LifeBoat. Let's call the pastor right now and set up an appointment for you. I'll go along too. I'll help you tell the pastor exactly what you said here."

Then I reach for the phone and make the call. I try not to let them back out of the hard conversation, because if they do, they'll usually go right back to complaining. In fact, if I'm able to get the pastor on the phone, I suggest he or she meet us right away. "Can you meet us for coffee right after this meeting? This is a very important issue to Sheila."

If the person is obviously set against the culture and direction of the church, I don't mind pointing that out. "Well, you know, this church isn't for everyone. There are plenty of churches in this town to choose from. You should probably look for one that is more in line with your vision for what a church should be."

I know one church whose goal was to reach non-believers. One woman kept complaining that she didn't want her kids in a youth group with un-Christian kids. Well, the leadership knew that if they had a youth group with only Christian kids, they would not be living up to their goals. So they had to tell the woman, "We're sorry, but this church isn't for everyone. In fact, non-believers are more welcome here than Christians who want a church with only Christians." She never did get it, but she did find another church.

Troubleshooting Tip No. 6
THE LIFEBOAT IS TOO BIG

Now here's a good problem to have: The LifeBoat has grown and is now too big. The living room you're meeting in is getting smaller every week. There's not enough parking at the Stewarts' apartment complex. I'm having trouble remembering the names of everyone's kids. Plus, how can our LifeGuard provide the care necessary for the life transformation of each individual when a group gets too large?

Personally, I think any boat over six people is too big. Not because of the size of our living rooms, though eight would be a squeeze, but because LifeBoats are about relationships — deep, trusting relationships. The bigger the group, the more impossible that becomes. As the old saying goes, the smaller the yacht, the better the sport.

A small-group ministry should be made up of *small* groups. Discussion does not flow as well in large groups. Sharing is not as free. Prayer time tends to be stiff.

Watch what happens when your Life-Boat breaks for refreshments. The crew mates will form small clusters. Why? Sharing works better in small clusters.

During discussion or prayer, try breaking your LifeBoat up. Put the men in the den and the women in the dining room, or some other combination.

It may be time to split the LifeBoat in two. Okay, we don't like to call it splitting, we prefer the term *multiplying*.

Let me save you some pain here. Dividing the group down the middle is heart-wrenching. An easier, less-painful method is when the LifeGuard and maybe one couple exits the crew to start a new Life-Boat. This leaves the First Mate to lead the original crew. Promotion! The First Mate is now a LifeGuard.

I'd suggest strongly that this new Life-Guard appoint a new First Mate quickly.

Launching the Fleet

Starting LifeBoats in Your Church

Now remember, this book is designed for the smaller church. So when we're talking about "launching a fleet," we're thinking a fleet of about four to ten LifeBoats.

Pray, Then Pray Some More

The place to start, of course, is on your knees. Prayer can do anything God can do. So pray and believe. Be very specific in your prayer. "Lord, show me who to start with. Help us cast the vision. We want to paint the future so that folks can see this in their mind's eye. Build an excitement. Point out the LifeGuards, the Bosun, the Stewards, and the First Mates..."

Cast Vision

Second, cast the vision. Talk to as many folks as possible over coffee, in the parking lot, in the hallway. Face-to-face, one-on-one meetings and to the whole congregation.

I preached three sermons on LifeBoats at one church, thinking I'd cast the vision and then once everyone knew what we were talking about, we could make some plans. But the congregation didn't wait for the plan. They just started forming their own LifeBoats. It took us months to catch up and find out what LifeBoats we had and who was leading what. Vision casting is very powerful. You put the vision out there and people just naturally start moving toward it.

Launching LifeGuards

Find and release some starter LifeBoats.

Eddie and I were talking the other day. We asked ourselves, "If we were both at the same church and both had a vision for LifeBoats, how would we get it started?"

Well, both of us are somewhat outgo-ing, therefore we would each start our own LifeBoat — so two LifeBoats. We would start small with, say, a crew of four. We'd slowly grow the crew, looking for someone with the gift of hospitality (a Steward) and someone with some leadership skills (a First Mate).

Then after training the First Mate and the Steward and growing the crew to six or eight, we'd leave the boat to their new leadership and go start another LifeBoat. But we'd both keep in contact with the first crew we started, talk to their new LifeGuard once or twice a month and attend one of their meetings at least once a quarter. Within a year, we'd have four LifeBoats, then six.

When somewhere between four and six LifeBoats had launched, we'd decide which one of us (Eddie or me) or whoever else would be the Bosun for that small fleet and start holding LifeGuard meetings every other month, also checking with the indi-vidual LifeGuards each month. The Bosun would then visit all the existing boats on a regular basis.

That would give us a good start. Then we'd build on the momentum.

Naval Academy

Form a LifeBoat of potential LifeGuards.

The Naval Academy is another way to launch a fleet. This is where you form a LifeBoat that trains potential LifeGuards. Invite four to eight leader types to your new LifeBoat/Naval Academy. You can either recruit only LifeGuards or pairs of LifeGuards and First Mates.

Over the next six to eight weeks, model LifeBoating for your LifeGuards. Run the

<blockquote>
"There is a thrill to launching a boat, a thrill that never dims in all the years to come.

—Phil Schwind
</blockquote>

meetings just like you'd run a LifeBoat meeting, with icebreakers, caring time, discussion, and vision casting. Between meetings, model how to be a LifeGuard. Check with your crew of LifeGuards, just like you'd do with a regular LifeBoat. Care for your crew. Get to know them. Celebrate their victories, birthdays, and anniversaries. Minister to them when they are hurting or sick. Model for them how to be a good LifeGuard.

The big difference would be that during the discussion time in your meetings, you'd talk about LifeBoats. You could use this book as your discussion guide perhaps. Of your six meetings, it might be good to use two for training, two for modeling, and two for empowering, by letting the trainees lead different parts of the meeting.

Commissioning

I grew up near the shipyard, and it was always a big deal whenever a ship was launched. Bigwigs from all over came

out for the occasion. Expensive bottles of champagne were broken across the bow and the ship slipped gently into the water. Then everyone waited with bated breath to see if it would float.

It's an excellent idea for churches to commission LifeGuards and LifeBoats with as much fanfare. This not only helps cast the vision of LifeBoating but also lets the LifeGuard and their LifeBoat know how important they are to the church.

Fishing Pond Events

Some churches hold regular Fishing Pond Events, where people who are not a part of a LifeBoat can come and explore (nibble at the bait). It's kind of like speed dating. The LifeGuards of new LifeBoats and those of crews that are open (at a point where new crew members would be welcome) are there to talk to potential shipmates. It's even better if the LifeGuards can bring some of their key crew members with them, so potential boaters can get a better idea of what each crew is like.

When someone marks on their connection card, or calls the church and asks, or mentions on their way out that they are interested in being in a LifeBoat, one of the Bosuns should supply them with a suggested list of LifeBoats that might fit their needs. A list of two or three would be fine. It would even be better if the Bosun chatted with them to find out what they are looking for in a LifeBoat, explain what LifeBoating is all about, or even arrange a time when the person can meet with the LifeGuards on the list. You might propose they visit all the LifeBoats on the suggested list (no more than three), so they can choose. Choosing gives them more buy-in.

LifeBoat Ahoy!

LifeBoating, what an adventure!

I hope by now you see clearly the necessity and the benefit of living life in a LifeBoat. I pray that you're excited about what real friendship can be — friendships in Christ.

The concept resonated recently with our friend Kyle:

I now understand why I'm not growing spiritually. I come to church faithfully every Sunday, but I come alone, I sit alone. Oh, I say hi to the greeter at the door. I shake hands with a few during the greeting time. I might smile at someone as I leave. But that's the extent of my friendships at church. They don't know me and I don't know them. I haven't allowed anyone close enough to really influence me, much less give me a little push in the right direction. Now I know why I'm not growing.

The light came on for him, and I'm praying that lots of you will see the light, too. I'm betting that you'll be curious enough to try LifeBoating. I believe that if you can only take the boat out for a bit of a row, you'll be hooked — a LifeBoat mariner for life. Once you've experienced being in an honest, open, caring, challenging, supporting LifeBoat ... it will be unthinkable to face the future without one.

You see, the Church is our ship. Now, people may book their tickets and come aboard to walk the decks and sample the sea life, but it's the LifeBoat that's made for exploration. It's the LifeBoat that can sail into small ports and uncharted coves. There is so much to see and so many people who need rescue.

So grab an oar. Set your course. And sail on, sailors! ◈

LIFEBOAT SURVIVAL STORY
"One Boat, Five Guys, Six Hours"

Now here's the story I promised you at the beginning of the book.

When I was a seminary student, I started meeting in the basement of the gym with four other guys. We were lifting weights and spotting each other.

The weight room was partitioned with two-by-fours and wrapped in chicken wire. It disturbingly resembled a cage. I think we were the only people who ever went down there, because it looked like it hadn't been dusted in fifteen years. Nevertheless, we met there three times a week — Monday, Wednesday, and Friday.

I don't remember who it was, but one day, one of us asked the others, "What do you want to be when you grow up?"

It was a funny question, because we were twenty-four at the time and considered ourselves already grown.

Bill answered, "I want to be a man of God."

After discussing this, we all came to the conclusion that we wanted to be men of God too. As the conversation continued, we realized that we could help each other do just that. Like we spotted each other lifting weights, we could get together and encourage each other to be what we wanted to be.

Who came up with the crazy idea to meet at 6 a.m. on Wednesday mornings, I don't know. But that's what we did. The president of the school even joined us about once a month.

Well, we got to know each other pretty well over time, and one day we decided to take a trip to the Outer Banks in North Carolina.

Tim had a boat — a very small boat — and we started to cross the sound over to Nags Head when trouble happened. The motor died when we were still in the middle of the channel.

We had no oars, but Tim said, "No problem. There's lots of boat traffic and somebody will be by to tow us in soon."

So we waited. One hour. Two hours. It was hot and we were thirsty ... and hungry. We didn't have provisions, because our plans included lunch on the other side.

By the fourth hour, I had thrown Bill out of the boat. The others pulled him back in.

It was six hours before we were rescued.

I don't know what happened in those six hours, but by the time the ordeal was over, we were a LifeBoat. We had crossed some invisible threshold; we weren't just weight-lifting buddies or prayer partners or preacher boys ... we were mates. Once out of that blasted broken boat in the sound, we were in another sturdier boat together and in it for life.

Made in the USA
Middletown, DE
23 July 2022

69762805R00060